INSIDE SOCIAL

Looking to the future

Helen Fitzhugh and Nicky Stevenson

First published in Great Britain in 2015 by

Policy Press
University of Bristol
1-9 Old Park Hill
Bristol
BS2 8BB
UK
t: +44 (0)117 954 5940
pp-info@bristol.ac.uk
www.policypress.co.uk

North America office:
Policy Press
c/o The University of Chicago Press
1427 East 60th Street
Chicago, IL 60637, USA
t: +1 773 702 7700
f: +1 773 702 9756
sales@press.uchicago.edu
www.press.uchicago.edu

British Library Cataloguing in Publication Data
A catalogue record for this book is available from the British Library

Library of Congress Cataloging-in-Publication Data
A catalog record for this book has been requested

ISBN 978 1 44731 035 8 paperback

Cover design by Qube Design Associates, Bristol
Printed and bound in Great Britain by CMP, Poole
Policy Press uses environmentally responsible print partners

Contents

Acknowledgements

Thank you to all of the interviewees who took the time to speak to us and share their views. We also thank all the staff supporting our interviewees. They were instrumental in helping us to make sure that the process of reviewing and amending the interview pieces happened smoothly and on time.

We would also like to thank Sally Kelly, Keith Bendell and Ann Nicholls, our former colleagues from The Guild who encouraged us at the very start of this book project.

A note on the information about interviewees and organisations in this book

The interviews for this project were carried out over the course of two years and the information about interviewees and organisations was collected at the time we wrote up the interview pieces. By the time this book comes to press, it is inevitable that some things will have changed. Some of the interviewees will have changed roles and organisations, while details of organisational membership or turnover will have changed. Therefore, please note that the descriptions of people and organisations in this book act to show the context for the interview at the time of writing, rather than the most up-to-date indication of what that person is doing today.

Glossary

An **asset lock** is a legal restriction on what can be done with an organisation's assets if it closes. Adopting an asset lock is a safeguard against the accrual of money and resources by an organisation purporting to work for the good of the community, only for those resources to then end up in private hands. This is seen as particularly important when the assets have been transferred out of public sector ownership in the first place. An asset lock exists in perpetuity.

Big Society was an idea put forward by the Conservatives during their 2010 election campaign aiming to promote ideas of localism, self-help, volunteering and government transparency.

Commissioning – often referred to in this book in relation to public service commissioning – is the act of defining what an organisation wants to buy in order to fulfil its goals. It is carried out by commissioners. Commissioning happens before procurement (see below).

Community development is a process of supporting people in specific communities or with particular interests to define issues that affect their lives, grow in confidence and work out practical ways of helping themselves and others in addressing those issues.

Community interest companies (CICs) were introduced as a new legal form for businesses with a social purpose under the Companies (Audit, Investigations and Community Enterprise) Act 2004. They must conform to particular legal requirements such as formal restrictions on the ability to transfer assets out of the organisation (an 'asset lock'), articles of association guaranteeing social purpose and restrictions on what would happen to the organisation if it closed. This model was developed by the Treasury, specifically to create opportunities for people to be able to earn interest from financial investment in social enterprises and for some of the business's profits to be paid in dividends. Both of these returns are capped within the original Act.

A **community share issue** takes place when a new community business needs capital to start up and asks members of the community to invest in it. Each community member who invests has a vote, regardless of the size of their investment, making the society democratic. They can withdraw their shares, but not transfer them, which makes the community shares different from shares in publically-owned companies which can pass from buyer to buyer regardless of their involvement in the business.

Co-operatives are businesses that are owned by members – often people who work for or buy from the co-op and therefore have a direct interest in its success. These members can influence how the co-op is run and receive a share of any profits. The term co-op does not refer to a specific legal structure, but instead to the family of organisations that follow **co-operative principles** such as voluntary and open membership, democratic control, economic participation by members, autonomy from outside control, educating members and the public about co-operation, co-operating with other co-ops and showing concern for the community.

Corporate social responsibility (CSR) refers to initiatives in mainstream businesses that either attempt to reduce the environmental harm of business operations, donate time or money to charitable causes or contribute in some way to the local community. The social activities are not the point of the business, as in social enterprises, but additional to them.

Credit unions are financial services providers owned and run by their members and often offer savings accounts and affordable credit to people who might otherwise find it hard to use conventional financial services.

Equity can refer to all the issued share capital of a company or to a shareholders' interest in that company.

Intermediate Labour Markets (ILMs) were organisations or programmes which provided short- to medium-term subsidised work experience and/or training to unemployed people in order to better their chances of re-entering the mainstream labour market.

Mem and Arts is an abbreviation of Memorandum and Articles of Association. These are the legal documents required when setting up a company which contain important information about the rules and regulations of how that company functions.

Mission drift is when an organisation starts up for one purpose but over time external influences or internal preferences alter or completely change that purpose. It is often referred to in relation to the effects of funder or investor requirements placed on charities or social enterprises to obtain income.

Mutuals are organisations owned by and run for the benefit of their members. There are no external shareholders.

Non-governmental organisations (NGOs) are organisations that do not operate for private profit and are not affiliated to governments or government agencies.

The **post-war social contract** represented a consensus across political parties that growth and restoration after the Second World War would be delivered through a capitalist economy but with the safeguards in place of greater social security, education and public health provision alongside state intervention in the economy where it was deemed necessary for the good of society.

Procurement is the act of purchasing goods or services that an organisation requires. It is carried out by procurement officers. It is often referred to in this book in relation to public services and is the process of obtaining the goods and services defined during commissioning, which is more about designing and specifying the services that are required. Procurement by public sector agencies is heavily regulated, in particular though European Union competition legislation.

Person-centred approaches to providing care and support place value on respecting the views of the person receiving support on what would help them most. This approach attempts to look at whole people in real-life situations, rather than focus simply on medical needs or issue labels.

Public service mutuals are organisations owned and/or managed by their staff, and which have contracts to deliver public services previously provided directly by national or local government or local health authorities.

The **Rochdale Pioneers** were a group of working people from Rochdale who set up a successful co-operative society in the 1840s which went on to serve as the template for the large UK and international co-operative movement that followed. The **Rochdale principles** of co-operation adopted by the society form the basis of the current international statement on co-operative identity (see co-operative principles above).

Social clauses in new tenders for services and products allow a local authority or other public agency to take into account the wider impact for the local community of the services or products they are commissioning. This stands in contrast to making purchasing decisions on the grounds of cost alone. Please also see the entry on the **Social Value Act 2012**.

A **social firm** is a market-led social enterprise set up specifically to create good quality jobs for people severely disadvantaged in the labour market.

The **Social Value Act 2012** is officially called the Public Services (Social Value) Act 2012 and contains a **social clause** stating that public authorities must consider the effect of any purchasing decisions they make on the economic, social and environmental well-being of the area in which they are operating.

Stakeholders are individuals, groups of people or other organisations that can affect, or be affected by, another organisation's actions and are therefore acknowledged to have an interest in the workings of that organisation. The use of the word 'stakeholder' contrasts with the word 'shareholder' to differentiate informal or undefined rights and responsibilities from the more orthodox focus on those of the official owners or investors in the organisations.

Stakeholder engagement is the process of giving stakeholders a say what goes on in an organisation. How deep the stakeholder engagement is depends on how much genuine influence the process allows stakeholders over important decision-making that affects them.

Third sector is a term used by some to refer to any organisations not in the mainstream business or public sectors – encompassing charities, social enterprises, co-ops, mutuals, voluntary associations and community groups.

The **Third Way** approach to politics in the UK is often associated with the rise of New Labour and the marriage of socialist principles of equality and community with the acceptance of more liberal ideas about capitalism.

The **triple bottom line** is a term that refers to judging the success of a business on its financial, social and environmental performance, in contrast to the usual (single) bottom line, which is financial.

A **Work Integration Social Enterprise (WISE)** focuses on improving employment prospects for those furthest from the labour market though a wider range of work-based opportunities.

ONE

Introduction: social enterprises today

Introducing social enterprises and this book

Twenty years ago, if you had asked most people what a social enterprise was, they would have had no idea what you were talking about. Maybe, after some thought, they would have had a vague notion that it is a business that does 'good things'. That is probably as far as you would have got. While it is still not a term that is used in general conversation, we have at least reached the stage where social enterprises can be mentioned on Radio 4 or the broadsheet newspapers in the UK without the need for detailed explanation.

Yet, as we shall explore in this book, there are still many different interpretations and strong opinions about what is, and what is not, a social enterprise. Political views, international cultural and economic contexts, personal beliefs and values and exposure to one particular type of social enterprise above others can undoubtedly influence these opinions. Nevertheless, it is possible to identify a range of 'good things' these diverse organisations have the potential to deliver. There is broad consensus on a list including some or all of the following:

- earning money through trading in order to generate money for good causes;
- creating jobs for people who might not get work in the mainstream labour market;
- helping local communities to take more control over what happens in their areas;
- enabling employees to own their own company and to participate in running it;

1

- enabling businesses to generate benefits for staff, customers and communities as well as investors.

While this list shows us what social enterprises might do, it also prompts further questions: in what ways are they similar and dissimilar to 'conventional' businesses? What kind of businesses can and can't be social enterprises? Who runs them? Who owns them? Who works for them? How many of them are there? And crucially – why should we be interested in them?

This book offers insight into how people who run, support, research and create policy around social enterprises currently set about answering these questions. It presents to readers who are either new to social enterprises, or who want to think about them more, the opportunity to hear directly from people who have thought deeply about social enterprises over a number of years. Hearing what these people are passionate about, what they value, what they are concerned about and what they want to change about how society currently works should help those new to social enterprise to start forming opinions about different social enterprise approaches and priorities. For those readers who already know about social enterprises, we hope the varied perspectives in this book will provide the basis for further questioning, developing and strengthening of opinions on what social enterprises could or should be in the future.

This approach is intentionally distinct from books and journal articles targeted at academic readers, which draw upon established bodies of research from different disciplines to respond to the questions listed above. While there are many excellent contributions to the study of social enterprise, their purpose is different and more geared towards building, testing and/or challenging theories or models for understanding social enterprises. We acknowledge that we have of course been influenced by current academic thinking as well as practice, policy and our own personal experiences (see Chapter Three 'About the Voices' for more on this) in developing our understanding of social enterprises. However, this book is different because it was conceived with the needs of a broader set of readers in mind. We hope that it will be of interest and practical use to people considering setting up or developing their own social enterprises, to people becoming involved in buying from or investing in social enterprises, and those beginning to study them.

Our aim is to raise awareness of the diversity of social enterprise approaches in plain, concise English. Crucially, though, we are not attempting to sell the idea of social enterprises uncritically. Instead we want to highlight the way that what is important to each reader – whether in terms of beliefs, values or political views – is important to each person's 'take' on social enterprises. By developing this understanding we hope to help people involved in social enterprises, or interested in them, to be clear about how their personal aims will affect how they do and (equally importantly) do not want to see social enterprises develop in the future.

This book looks back and it looks forward. The longest chapter comprises interviews with people who run, support, research or have an influence on social enterprises. These provide diverse views on what social enterprises are, could be, or should be in the future. In doing so, they highlight current and cutting edge thinking. We are given privileged access to the ideas social enterprise practitioners are working on *now*, which will inform the *future* of the sector. The final chapter of this book will highlight different motivations and approaches from the interviews and offer ways of thinking about how these differences influence the predictions we can make about the future of social enterprises.

The rest of this introduction will provide a basic overview of the subject of social enterprise, drawing on understandings developed since the rise of the co-op movement, in order to help those new or relatively new to the idea of social enterprise to make the most of the interviews. In short, we look back to build a foundation in the Introduction and then we look forward to build upon it in Chapter Four on the Voices. We start by trying to explain what a social enterprise is.

What is a social enterprise?

Whatever debates there are about the nature of social enterprises (and there are many), everyone agrees that they *are* involved in more than just making money. The only trouble is that people don't always agree what that 'more' could or should be.

At the most basic level, social enterprises are organisations which:

- sell goods or services to obtain at least some of their income;
- carry out activities that are socially or environmentally beneficial;
- write their governing documents in a way that makes clear the social intent behind the business (to benefit people and/or the environment).

Additionally, some social enterprises emphasise that they:

- do not distribute their profits for private benefit;
- are owned by people who have a stake in the business, such as working in it, buying from it or living in the local community.

Earned income

The fact that social enterprises sell goods and/or services to gain income makes them businesses. However, not all social enterprises gain all of their income from sales – for instance, some also take gifts of money or goods in the form of grants or donations.

One of the key debates about social enterprises is therefore – how much of an organisation's income has to be *earned* (by selling goods and services) rather than *donated* before it can be called a social enterprise? Some people want to define a percentage of income that must be earned before an organisation can be defined as such. Others suggest being a social enterprise is more about the spirit of how the organisation operates – that is to say, how 'entrepreneurially' it approaches the process of income generation.

Socially beneficial activities

For some, the 'social' in social enterprise means that the business activity sets out to achieve outcomes that benefit disadvantaged people and/or the environment. An example of this would be a business that employs mainly long-term unemployed people in order to give them the experience and confidence that will help them enter or return to mainstream employment. For others, the 'social' means that the business is run in a way that challenges mainstream business practice and transfers power from traditional owners and investors (usually the powerful in society) to groups of people whom the business actually affects. These would include people who work in the business or those who buy or benefit from its goods and services. An example of this is **co-operatives** where people who buy from a business (in the case of a consumer co-op) or work for a business (in the case of a worker co-op) own it and therefore control it and are able to benefit from its profits. There is also a view that the 'social' element should include both *how* they operate and *the type of results they achieve.*

Of course, it is important to recognise that mainstream businesses benefit society hugely. They are the means of providing food, utilities, clothing, shelter and jobs to people. New products allow for and encourage changes in culture and social interaction. At its most basic level, capitalism is based on the idea that competition to make money out of people's needs, will best meet those needs. All of this means that it is important to understand what it is that makes social enterprises different from mainstream businesses. The distinction arises in the organisation's purpose for being.

'Social' intent drives the business

People new to social enterprise often ask how it relates to **corporate social responsibility** (CSR). Many mainstream companies operate CSR programmes that actively support 'good causes' – from local schools to global health initiatives. Some act as a positive influence in their local community by sponsoring a local park, training young people in the area or paying for the Christmas lights. What is at issue in comparing mainstream businesses to social enterprises is not whether these CSR activities contribute to society by providing socially beneficial activities. Instead, the distinction relates to intent and purpose. What makes social enterprises different is that their very purpose for being is to deliver on their social mission. Running a business that trades in goods or services is simply the *means* by which they achieve this. This intent should be written into the organisation's governing documents and any mission statements and strategic plans, in order for the organisation to be defined as a social enterprise. In short, the social purpose is their reason for being and a business approach is the means of delivering that.

This contrasts with the benefits arising from running mainstream businesses and their CSR initiatives. Generally, the purpose of the business is to make financial profit in order to distribute it to the owners – either the private owners or the people who trade in and speculate on the changes in value of public shares. Any social benefit (whether financial or non-financial in nature) provided to other people affected by the organisation (usually termed **stakeholders**) does not alter the profit-making purpose of the organisation, but comes about as a side benefit. However large and successful any CSR initiative is, it could be dropped at any moment by a mainstream business because it is not integral to the organisation's purpose for being. Similarly, the provision of jobs in large mainstream firms is determined by the requirement for workers to help create profit for the owners and shareholders, rather than because the primary purpose of the business is to create jobs.

The issue of intent is fundamental. Mainstream businesses can and do change the nature of their trading activities and other commitments to pursue increased profits. Yet if a social enterprise stopped trying to deliver on its social purpose and just followed whatever activity would make the most money, it would no longer be a social enterprise.

What happens to the profits?

There is a view that the profits social enterprises make from selling goods and/or services should only ever be re-invested in developing the business itself or furthering the social mission (rather than being distributed to owners and investors as in conventional businesses). On the other hand, others believe that a minimal amount of profit-distribution to investors is fine and in fact necessary to encourage more growth in social enterprises. In co-operatives where the point is to distribute the profits to a different set of people than usual (for example the everyday customers rather than shareholders speculating on the value of shares) the 'social-ness' of the use and distribution of profit is viewed differently by different commentators depending on their idea of what constitutes a social good. Some think that in order for the business to be a social enterprise, those benefiting from profit-distribution in this way should be poorer or more disadvantaged members of the community. Others say that the 'social' part stems from changing flows of power and money in society and that profits can be distributed to general consumers or workers on the basis of equality and democratic business structures.

How the UK government defines social enterprises

The official UK government definition of social enterprise has remained the same under successive governments since 2002:

> A social enterprise is a business with primarily social objectives whose surpluses are principally reinvested for that purpose in the business or in the community, rather than being driven by the need to maximise profit for shareholders and owners. (DTI, 2002, 8)

It is significant that it includes words like 'primarily' and 'principally' when discussing the organisation's purpose and process of profit-distribution, rather than absolutes. While in some other countries there is a legal definition of co-operatives and social enterprises, UK governments of all political persuasions have opted for a laissez-faire approach to the debate on definitions. Although the Labour government in the 1990s attempted to include CSR in its definition of social enterprise and in 2010 a minister in the coalition government referred to NHS health trusts as social enterprises, ongoing debate between practitioners has generally resisted the inclusion of parts of the private and public sectors. This still leaves plenty of disputed space occupied by a wide range of organisations.

Clearing up confusion: social enterprises or social entrepreneurship?

'Social enterprise', 'social entrepreneurs' and 'social entrepreneurship' have often been treated as if they were interchangeable. Yet as interest in alternative ways of providing social change has grown, these terms have developed different meanings (Defourney, 2009). While these are (as ever with social enterprise issues) disputed, we offer our own take – informed by the latest thinking and our own experiences – below.

For us, the term 'social enterprises' refers specifically to *organisations*: those businesses that are driven by and carry out a social purpose. 'Social enterprise' (without the plural) can get a little more confusing. We use it uncontroversially in this book to mean one social enterprise organisation, but we occasionally also use it to signify the whole movement of organisations that trade for a social purpose. However, we do not take it to mean the same thing as social entrepreneurship – although it clearly has many overlaps. We did not limit the interviewees in our books to our thinking. If we asked them about social enterprises and they responded by referring to what we see as social entrepreneurship, we included their response as we were equally as interested in where their thinking would take them in the future.

Social entrepreneurship is often talked about in a broader context. It can be seen as a process of acting innovatively to try to effect social change in the public sector, in mainstream businesses, in associations and protest groups, as well as in social enterprises (Nicholls, 2008). Some people are not happy with this broader usage as it is sometimes used to suggest that any organisation operated by a social entrepreneur is de facto a social enterprise. If you accept the defining characteristics given earlier (particularly the need for earned income or the idea that you can't distribute profits from a social enterprise to private investors, for instance), then it becomes clear why people who find those particular elements of social enterprises most important are likely to resist the idea that everything achieved through social entrepreneurship is a social enterprise. To avoid the focus on 'entrepreneurship', some people refer to the even broader idea of 'social innovation', or put simply: developing new products, services or approaches to addressing social problems (Lettice and Parekh, 2010).

Social entrepreneurs are people who practice social enterpreneurship. They don't have to be individuals acting in isolation, groups can also act in this way. However, for some in the social enterprise sector, focusing on social entrepreneurs as individuals, rather than on the organisations they create, can be worrying because it takes the focus away from older forms of organising that emphasise acting in groups with solidarity. Also, some people say that not all social enterprises are 'entrepreneurial' (in the sense of taking risk and doing things differently) so it is, for instance, not appropriate automatically to assume that you can call the manager of a social enterprise a social entrepreneur.

Muhammad Yunus – founder of the Grameen Bank and joint winner of the Nobel Peace Prize for bringing accessible small loans to the poor of Bangladesh – often refers to 'social business' and sees this as a better term than 'social enterprise' (Yunus and Weber, 2010).

We stick to the more commonly used 'social enterprise' because we feel that it has been better defined and it is used in UK policy and practice, but again, we were happy to hear from interviewees who preferred the other term when we interviewed them.

There are all sorts of other ideas that are related to the types of activity described above. For instance, people are increasingly interested in social investment, social marketing, community enterprise, bottom of the pyramid enterprises, fair trade, the social economy, the solidarity economy and at the broadest level – new and 'human' economics movements.

Broadly speaking – using the terms already explained above – social investment and social marketing are forms of social innovation. Community enterprises, bottom of the pyramid enterprises and fair trade organisations can fall clearly within some definitions of social enterprise but might be disputed by others (for instance a bottom of the pyramid enterprise sells low cost items to the global poor and makes its profit that way – it might benefit the poor greatly to have access to those items, but if the profits are then only distributed to rich investors in a rich country, some people might say that the way that it is organised is not social enough to count as a social enterprise). Social enterprises are part of the social economy and if they involve a political and collective awareness they might also be seen as part of the solidarity economy. New and 'human' economics movements stress the importance of organising our global and national economies with people and the environment in mind, rather than just profit and self-interest. (We recommend Hart et al, 2010 for further clear and detailed information on all of these topics.)

Philanthropy and self-help

The earliest manifestation of social enterprise in Britain was the growth of the co-operative movement in the 1830s and 1840s as a corrective to some of the excesses of the industrial revolution. Initially developed by philanthropic factory owners, often influenced by religious beliefs, innovators such as Robert Owen tried to improve the working and living conditions of their employees. The first co-operative shop was opened in Rochdale in 1844 to enable industrial workers to buy cheap and unadulterated food. The co-operative movement challenged the power base of the conventional company by sharing ownership with the people who produced or purchased the goods and services.

The co-operative and self-help or mutual model continues to be the favoured approach in mainland Western Europe in which social enterprises are seen as a force for social change. In some Western European countries, there is a legal definition of a co-operative or social enterprise and they are overseen to ensure that these organisations fulfil their roles as socially beneficial organisations. Tax benefits are available in some countries to reward the benefits social enterprises produce for society.

Meanwhile, the philanthropic tradition, in which those with wealth and resources are encouraged by their religious beliefs or a social conscience to provide support for the poor and disadvantaged, has been recognised since the seventeenth century when the first definition of charities was written into law. Charities, unlike social enterprises, are clearly defined, regulated in the UK by the Charity Commission and granted advantageous tax status, operationally and to incentivise donations from organisations and individuals. As a result of this long tradition and a clear definition, charities are recognised globally as organisations that operate for social benefit.

The two traditions of philanthropy and self-help evolved in the UK throughout the twentieth century. Some charities began campaigning to change the conditions that caused the problems they were called on to address. In the 1960s a practice called **community development** was established, in which local people and external agencies tried to empower themselves to be able to influence the planning and other decisions made by government – for instance around the post-war housing developments.

For many casual observers the loose association of organisations that 'do good things' in society has often been vaguely associated with the notion of philanthropy, more than with the other approaches described above. Yet, the concept of social enterprise can be traced back to traditions of philanthropy, mutuality and community development.

The final influencing factor in the shaping the UK social enterprise sector was the social entrepreneur model, well-established in the United States but pioneered in the UK by Michael Young when he set up the School for Social Entrepreneurs in 1997. The social entrepreneurship model prioritises the individual entrepreneur as the agent of change. This can include dynamic and entrepreneurial individuals working in their communities, but also increasingly recognises the role of entrepreneurial thinking in public sector organisations to reform what some see as bureaucratic systems that are slow to adapt to the current needs of society.

Since the 1980s many charities operating in the traditional voluntary sector have earned some of their income through trading. Following the Labour government's adoption of a social enterprise strategy in 2002, some of these organisations started to define themselves as social enterprises. In the face of the economic crisis and public sector funding cuts from 2008 onwards, grant funding to the voluntary sector has been reduced, which has also acted as an incentive to voluntary organisations to generate income through delivering contracted services.

Organisations set up from the start as social enterprises have challenged whether voluntary organisations can honestly be called enterprises and whether they have made the required cultural and organisational changes to operate as businesses. Some voluntary and community organisations have specifically resisted these changes as a threat to their ethos and values. The debates about whether philanthropic organisations could, or should, transition into social enterprises has long been a contentious one and has been extensively covered elsewhere (for example Palmer and Mornement, 2005; McKay et al, 2011; Chew and Lyon, 2012; Teasdale et al, 2013a; Dey and Teasdale, 2013). Those who are interested in social enterprises primarily as a means of supplementing and/or replacing the income of charitable and voluntary organisations can be described as operating within the 'earned income' school of thought about social enterprise (Defourney and Nyssens, 2010).

While the debate about the role of trading in charitable and voluntary organisations is an important one, this book intentionally looks at social enterprises from a much broader perspective. This is in recognition that the 'earned income' perspective is not the only way of thinking about social enterprises. The work of the EMES Network in Europe has involved careful description and reflection on what constitute social enterprises. A paper written by two key contributors to the network contrasts the 'earned income' school to the 'social innovation' school (which focuses on social outcomes created by a flexible and innovative approach to social change-making) and to

EMES' own approach (Defourney and Nyssens, 2010). The EMES approach is interested in the economic and social change dimensions of social enterprises covered by the other approaches, but also includes explicit reference to how they are governed and owned and whether they provide opportunities for democratic control and participation.

So, while one question to be asked about social enterprises is 'what role could they and should they play in offering an alternative source of income for voluntary and community organisations?', it is vital to recognise that this is not the only important question to ask about social enterprises.

Social enterprises and government

When the idea for this book was first tentatively proposed in 2011, **Big Society** was one of the flagship agendas for the Conservatives entering power (in coalition with the Liberal Democrats). Social enterprises and **public service mutuals** were considered part of an approach to addressing social problems involving self-help and community spirit, under the somewhat vaguely defined concept of Big Society.

While the idea of social enterprises as independent deliverers of hitherto publicly run services has not gone away (and is discussed by many in this book), by the time of coming to print, the term Big Society had all but disappeared. Yet the fact that the Conservatives had seen social enterprises as compatible with their agenda is interesting because just a couple of years before that the Labour government had seen them as equally suitable vehicles for progressing their own **Third Way** goals. For instance, social enterprise approaches were encouraged by Blair's New Labour government, with regard to the regeneration agenda, where policies focused on revitalising disadvantaged communities. Later the same Labour government also referenced social enterprises in their social inclusion and empowerment policies. One key action taken by Labour was to launch **Community Interest Companies** as a new business model for social enterprises, principally to encourage financial investment.

Looking further back, even before the widespread use of the term social enterprise, the Conservative governments of the 1980s and early 1990s had funded Co-operative Development Agencies as part of the process of encouraging business start-ups and business ownership – all of which shows how appealing the social enterprise concept can be to both ends of the political spectrum.

While many and indeed most social enterprises have grass-roots, non-governmental origins, this attention and occasional financial support from government sources (for instance financial support to regional social enterprise infrastructure organisations and money for programmes to encourage social enterprise start-ups) has lead to debates about how involved or close to government social enterprise should be. While it has been suggested that contributing to government agendas is a sound way to influence policy to gain opportunities and legitimacy, there is also a view that it eventually leads to **mission drift** and a lack of independence and sustainability when the political winds change. Consequently there is concern that those who oppose the externalisation of public services will become hostile to social enterprises in general, seeing them as the 'acceptable face' of privatisation.

One key to the controversy of changing the nature of public service delivery

Philanthropic activity is by nature top-down: people who have more giving to those who have less. Mutuality is bottom-up: people sharing democratic control over mutually beneficial activities.

It would appear that some policymakers are attracted to the idea of philanthropy because it represents people within society looking after others without the mediation of government or the use of government funds. The natural end to this thinking is that altruism will provide public services rather than taxation. However, this point of view is controversial, because the government is held accountable through democratic public elections for the use of taxes to provide public services. In contrast, the governance of philanthropic organisations through trustee boards is essentially private. While some community-led social enterprises recruit directors openly, making the delivery of services directly accountable to users, it is still only the state that has ultimate responsibility for money raised through taxation. Those who favour philanthropic organisations because they exist outside government also place social enterprises within a market place that will self-regulate to ensure that if they do not respond to needs, the mechanisms of the market will mean that they lose contracts to be replaced by more efficient service providers.

In contrast, mutuality is the adoption of group governance. Organisations working in mutual or co-operative ways and delivering public services could potentially provide a different type of democratic control to five-yearly elections – making it a more local and immediate type of accountability. The difference lies in the extent to which **mutuals** adopt features of representative or of participative democracy. In representative democracy, the decisions are taken by leaders elected by the community – so the contribution the community members make is to choose a representative who will speak for them. In participative democracy the contribution the community members make is to participate in discussions of issues for themselves in a less hierarchical system of representation and to become directly involved in decision-making. This becomes more direct because it has not been delegated to others, but is also more time-consuming for those involved. A more participative approach would rely on citizens becoming far more involved and engaged in many different types of local activity than the current system of taxation and public services demands.

Some also suggest that any approach to outsourcing public service provision that transfers control from government to organisations or communities would damage the universality of public service provision, because each local area would decide on different approaches and priorities.

One of the key questions about social enterprises has therefore become, what role could they and should they play in providing social welfare and local services and when is it more appropriate for the state to remain in control? This topic is amply debated in the chapters that follow.

A blurred picture of the social enterprise sector in the UK

As this discussion has undoubtedly shown, the social enterprise sector in the UK has been defined in many different ways, by diverse sets of people, in accordance with the expectations of different agendas and priorities. All of this ambiguity has meant that although people are increasingly interested in social enterprises, there is still much we cannot say about the size and state of the sector.

In policy documents and some research papers, commonly cited figures from the Annual Survey of Small Businesses allowed researchers to suggest that there was a large UK social enterprise sector (55,000) in 2005 and that it was growing (62,000 in 2007 and 70,000 in 2012). However, a recent critique of these figures suggested that the definitions used to obtain them varied considerably and were influenced by political considerations. On the grounds of legal structure alone, the paper claimed that up to 90 per cent of each of these totals could be considered private businesses (Teasdale et al, 2013b). It also identified that a later survey conducted along different lines (examining the proportion of voluntary, community and civil society organisations that could be considered social enterprises) suggested a figure of around 16,000 social enterprises in the UK (Teasdale et al, 2013b). This further piece of research also had its limitations, in that the research methodology could have potentially missed social enterprises embedded more in the business environment than the **third sector**. While a range of organisations accept and publicise different accounts, it is fair to say that the problem of defining what is and is not a social enterprise has so far dogged attempts to gain an indisputable picture of the size and scope of the social enterprise sector in the UK.

The State of Social Enterprise Survey 2013 was carried out on behalf of Social Enterprise UK (SEUK), the infrastructure body for social enterprises in the UK. It involved a largely random sample from a population of around 9,000 organisations identified as social enterprises for the purposes of this research, due to their membership of SEUK and other infrastructure bodies. Findings drawn from this survey suggested the relative youth of the sector, with around a third of all social enterprises having only been established in the previous three years. It also evidenced that most (not all) social enterprises were small or micro enterprises. Three-quarters of the respondents were earning over 75 per cent of their income from trade.

Support and membership organisations such as Co-operatives UK, Social Firms UK and the Social Enterprise Mark also map and provide evidence about their own relevant types of social enterprise. For instance, in 2013 Co-operatives UK research found that there were over 6,000 co-operatives in the UK, with a total turnover of £36.7 billion. Over 300 social enterprises have applied and qualified for the Social Enterprise Mark. This requires them to evidence their independence as an organisation, their social and/or environmental aims, that at least 50 per cent of their income is from trading and at least 50 per cent of the profits are spent on fulfilling their social aims – as well as demonstrating that they provide some kind of social value (for more about the Social Enterprise Mark see Lucy Findlay's interview in Chapter Four). **Social firms** are social enterprises specifically focused on providing good quality jobs for people who would otherwise find it hard to enter the labour market. In 2010, at the last point of mapping the sector, around 100 established social firms were identified and just under that number again were identified as working towards the goal of operating as social firms.

Social enterprises: why should we be interested in them?

The world of social enterprise is complicated. The obvious question is then: why should people be interested in a slightly confusing, relatively small phenomenon (at least so far in the UK) called social enterprise, especially when even the people within the sector cannot entirely agree what it is all about? That question is exactly what the following interview pieces on the future of social enterprise are able to answer.

By asking social enterprise practitioners, supporters, thinkers and policy-makers what they think will happen with these types of business in the future, this book reveals the depth and innovation in the thinking behind individual and specific social enterprise activities carried out currently in the UK. By stepping outside everyday considerations of keeping their organisations afloat and asking their founders, managers and supporters to consider their wider goals, this book offers the opportunity to see how ideas tested out and refined in these organisations could influence thinking on topics as widespread and important as global capitalism, social welfare provision, the future of the voluntary and community sector, environmental sustainability, worker satisfaction and democratic representation.

One of the particular reasons to be interested in social enterprises is because they offer a different reason and set of values for doing business. It has been suggested that since the global financial crisis of 2008 the public has become much more aware of the role of businesses in their lives. Media tales of corporate mismanagement, tax avoidance, appalling working conditions in developing countries and charges of collaboration with national security services in order to facilitate public surveillance have kept the ethics of capitalism at the forefront of people's minds. The Occupy movement was a visible demonstration of this concern. In response, even the most mainstream business journals such as the *Harvard Business Review* are publishing articles referring to the need for all businesses to engage in the creation of 'shared value' for a range of different stakeholders (Porter and Kramer, 2011) and for leaders to adopt 'higher ambition' in helping businesses achieve a wider set of benefits for society (Foote et al, 2011) This means that there has never been a better time to learn from social enterprises: businesses that already have extensive experience of benefiting more than one set of stakeholders at once while balancing the books. This book suggests that it is possible to learn from these organisations – their successes and their failures – to help shape the future of capitalism.

TWO

From the sidelines to the mainstream? Two personal introductions to social enterprise

Nicky Stevenson set up a social enterprise consultancy called The Guild in 1991 with her colleague Sally Kelly. In 2008, Helen Fitzhugh came to work for them as a researcher. Helen and Nicky both left The Guild in 2012 with a commitment to carry on working together on this book.

Nicky's view

Twenty years of social enterprise development. It's only when you stop and look back that you realise the progress that has been made. It's important to discuss this progress before we listen to the Voices in this book describe what could and should happen in the next 20 years. What has been done hasn't been easy and it is important to ask if it had to be this difficult and to ask if we could have gone further? Looking back, there is a lot of ground to cover and perhaps the best way is to identify some key moments.

In April 1985 I started work at the Norfolk and Norwich Co-operative Development Agency (CDA), first as a researcher and then as a business adviser. It was important to me because I met Sally Kelly, with whom I would work for the next 26 years and because I became involved in the weird world of 1980s co-op development. CDAs were popular both with the Conservative government and with local authorities of all political persuasions. The Tories liked us because we promoted enterprise and would help to reduce unemployment.

Labour councils liked us because of the traditional party links with the co-op sector. We were seen as an alternative to capitalism, red in tooth and claw. The movement attracted a lot of fellow travellers, people who wanted to advise or run co-ops because they were non-hierarchical alternatives to the mainstream, rather more than they wanted to run a business that needed to make a profit. However, a lot of people who worked in CDAs went on to form the bedrock of **community development**, social enterprise, micro-finance and a whole load of other ways of creating sustainable economic development in the following 20 years.

In spite of odd training sessions that involved us all linking arms and taking our shoes off and constantly moving furniture out of hierarchical lines into co-operative circles, we developed a robust methodology of how to set up and run businesses that traded for social and environmental purpose as well as making money. In 1992, when the Rio Earth Summit created a definition of sustainability as a three-legged stool consisting of finance, the environment and the social or community, all we had to do was nod and carry on – these values already underpinned what we did. By now the CDA had closed, a victim of local government cuts, and Sally and I set up our own business: The Guild. We had to explain our strap line 'consultants to the social economy' to everyone we met. It was a term we had adopted from mainland Europe, describing the intersection of social and economic activity. We discovered that because of our experience in the CDA we knew how to do things that few people in the wider voluntary and charity sector understood at the time. We knew how to bid for European funding, how to cost services that were being put out to Compulsory Competitive Tender and how to set up trading arms of charities. When the government of the day started to roll out place-based regeneration initiatives we knew how to work in poor communities and help to empower local residents to take control of these programmes and have a say in what was still being done *to* them by governments.

It wasn't easy to do. Frequently local government officers and other public servants were reluctant to let go of decision making powers. Local politicians thought that councils were the right organisations to run things, recognising only representative democracy as a legitimate and accountable basis for spending money. At best they paid lip service to participative democracy. Nevertheless, by the mid-1990s some large and influential organisations, such as the WISE group in Glasgow, were established as **Intermediate Labour Markets**, paving the way for social enterprises as we know them today. At first, it felt like the general election result of 1997 was going to provide a fair wind to help the whole movement to set sail. It quickly became clear, however, that the Labour government, like its predecessors and successor, thought it had the right to redefine who we were and what we were doing. We had a new Social Enterprise Unit at the Department of Trade and Industry, but immediately we had a fight on our hands as the published definition of social enterprise included businesses that give to charity as an optional extra. The formation of a national Social Enterprise Coalition in 2002 gave us a platform from which to debate these issues and offer our own definitions.

It became clear that the social enterprise movement included different models trying to do different things. **Social firms** exist to create job opportunities for people who would struggle in the mainstream labour market; development trusts build assets in communities that are owned and controlled by local people, co-operatives are still in the picture, creating alternative ways of owning and running the economy. A new model called the **Community Interest Company** was launched in 2005 as a company structure legally required to remain in community ownership but also able to generate investment and pay dividends – in addition to the existing co-op structures. All of these organisations earn at least part of their income through trading and all of them reinvest their profits for a social purpose. Some of us feel that no government has seriously addressed the question of beneficial taxation to incentivise people to set up or convert their businesses to social enterprises. They have all been too reluctant to legislate to say that this is a social enterprise and this isn't. So within the sector we keep having to have the discussion, over and over and over again.

Working with partners in other European Union countries gave some of us the opportunity to experience how **co-operatives** and social enterprises can be embedded in the economy. Visiting Emilia Romagna in northern Italy opened our eyes when we asked directors of a large housing co-operative if they had rules that meant they had to commission building and other work from co-operatives. "No," they said, looking baffled. It took us a while to realise that there were so many building and service co-ops in the local economy that they didn't need to think about whom they bought from.

We have still got a long way to go. As we have worked on this book, the economy has been suffering as a result of banks collapsing and the consequent global economic crisis. Sadly, at the time when it has been most needed, the Co-operative Bank has experienced its own problems with governance and attempting to grow through taking over other institutions. But as one of our contributors pointed out – did that happen because it was behaving too much like a co-operative or too much like a bank? You could draw the conclusion that we need to strengthen our co-ops as alternatives to the mainstream, not dilute them to the point where they behave like everyone else. We should also remember that the co-op movement in Britain is far bigger than the Co-operative Group (the national umbrella body for the Co-op shops, the bank, insurance service, funeral care, etc.), consisting of individual worker and consumer co-ops, **credit unions**, local co-op societies and the many affiliated organisations such as Co-operative Women's Guilds and the Woodcraft Folk.

The environment, the economy, the community. These are all equally important and the social enterprise sector will thrive if it maintains this balance. But in order to do this it needs to grow and in this book, important Voices explain how and why this will happen. And my vision of the future does come back to co-operatives. Later on in that visit to Emilia Romagna, we were visiting a social co-operative, sitting on the side of a hill outside a fifteenth-century villa converted into residential care for adults with learning disabilities, jointly owned by their families. Below us were vineyards and a market garden where the residents worked to feel valued and useful and to earn some of the income to keep the co-op running. One of our Italian colleagues was describing how this part of Italy was the centre of the country's co-operative movement and gestured to the valley below. "This", he said "is Rochdale." We knew what he meant. It is a source of pride that the world looks to the UK for models of value-based business, based on fairness, equality and caring for others. Whether they are co-operators or not, our Voices prove that this tradition is alive and well and, if they have their way, will be bigger and better in the future.

Nicky Stevenson
February 2014

Helen's view

I have only been thinking about and researching social enterprises as long as I've known Nicky and Sally. So, when Nicky describes her own experiences in the sector, she is also describing a point of view which has had a major influence on my own understanding.

When I first went to work for Nicky and Sally, I moved from a job researching the outcomes of voluntary and community initiatives and educational programmes. I'd previously worked for public sector organisations, a foundation and volunteered for a couple of charities. So by the time I started at The Guild I thought that I already had a reasonable understanding of ways of working for social good. Yet, attending one of my colleague's training sessions, soon after starting at The Guild, did much to highlight the gaps in my experience.

It was not so much the content of the 'Introduction to social enterprise' session that sticks in my mind. Instead of focusing on the novelty of the business for social purpose concept or the practicalities of following it through, what I remember most is the attitude of everyone around me on the course. These people were interested in social enterprises because they were trying to make a difference in the world. They were creatively searching for alternatives that would bring in enough income to fund new ways of helping people and empowering communities. I found their enthusiasm and their willingness to go out and directly generate the money they needed incredibly refreshing. Especially impressive were those who were trying to address 'unfashionable' but entrenched social problems where little political or even public charitable support could usually be found. They were thinking up new products and ways of doing things in areas that traditional businesses deemed unprofitable.

I found the atmosphere of possibility exciting then, and even after years of seeing how challenging and involved a process translating that enthusiasm into viable businesses can be, I still do. I am a researcher because I believe that systematic and responsible curiosity about the world informs actions that improve human life. How lucky I am, then, to have found organisations to research that embody that aim too.

Helen Fitzhugh
February 2014

THREE

About the Voices

The following chapter contains just under 40 separate 'Voices'. We interviewed people about what social enterprise could or should do in the near distant future – working with the figure of approximately 20 years from now to help people focus their thinking. The interviewees were people who run social enterprises, who research and think about social enterprises, who make policy that affects social enterprises and who support and raise awareness of social enterprises.

From our previous experience and understanding of social enterprises, we knew that whatever else might come up in these discussions, the future visions we were asking for would be very different for each person. People's visions would depend on their personal definitions and their experiences. The interviewees were picked by us specifically for the breadth and range of their interests and experiences, to illuminate the range of thinking on doing business for a social purpose or in a social way, rather than to provide a representative or more generalisable mapping of views across the sector. This openness seemed to us essential when discussing something as unpredictable as the future. Our selection of interviewees was therefore made on the basis of diversity and was informed by our previous experience in the sector and by the advice of key informants from social enterprise support organisations. We also selected on the basis of people's long-term experience in the social enterprise sector, which is why people running very new social enterprises have not been included in our sample.

We decided not to conduct this research process in what might be considered a more traditional way, by collecting together all of the interview transcripts, systematically going through them to identify common themes and then presenting our discussion and conclusions using excerpts of text to illustrate them. Instead, we wanted each contribution to retain its distinctiveness and for the interviewees themselves to retain power over how their voices were used. This meant co-creating the texts with the interviewees to make sure they were happy with how their voices were being represented.

We did this in the following way:

- by starting each interview with the same set of broad questions (see Appendix Two), but allowing the interviewees the freedom to explore particular points that interested them more than others and to answer in the context of their own organisations or in relation to a particular model of social enterprise;
- by taking notes during the interviews, summarising our interpretation of the key points arising in her or his point of view and checking these with the interviewee immediately at the end of the interview to gain agreement or correction straight away;
- by writing up the key points from the interviewees, with substantial quotes, and sending the text to the interviewees with confirmation that they had complete freedom to accept, amend or make larger revisions to the text.

Some interviewees were happy with the texts as they stood, some required more work in order to make sure they conveyed exactly the points they wanted to make.

The stories you are about to read are the product of this process. We have loosely grouped these into sections, in the hope of providing snapshots of particular areas of agreement or disagreement within the sector and of interesting parallels in different people's views. Many other groupings could have been chosen, but we hope that the following will provide an interesting narrative thread and therefore a readable set of stories.

If you would like to know a little more about why and how we gathered together these Voices, please find more detail below.

Our approach

This book started life as a simple question: 'What is it all for?' We were working with and for social enterprises at the time and there was a lot of frustration in the sector about definitions, about policy and about what the changing political climate (from Labour to a Conservative-Liberal Democrat coalition in 2010) would mean for social enterprises. A lot of the discussion seemed to us, at that particular moment, to be focused on day-to-day concerns and survival. While this may have been necessary, it did not seem sufficient to help people think clearly about why a social enterprise approach might or might not be useful for the future. The idea of this book was to lift us out of the minutiae of current policy, pragmatism and strategic positioning and to create a space to think about what was really important. The specific question that formed the foundation of this research process was 'What could or should social enterprises do for the quality of life of people in the UK in the near distant future?' We acknowledge the framing of this question grew from our own involvement in the UK social enterprise sector, particularly working with social enterprises involved in providing services and employment to disadvantaged people and in organising co-operatively. Our aim was to contribute to and stimulate the debate on the long-term and wide-ranging purposes of these types of social enterprise approaches, in contrast to the local and detailed discussions of the form that were going on in policy and practice circles at the time.

When we started this process we wanted to uncover assumptions and hopes for the impact social enterprises could or should have on people's lives. While a number of our interviewees also discussed environmental benefits of social enterprises, our choice of interviewees did not encompass the full range of environmentally-motivated social enterprises in the UK. This was because the choice was informed by the desire to find diverse answers to the question of social enterprise's direct impact on people's well-being and development, rather than through indirect means such as improving the environment. While we acknowledge the importance of environmental causes as a legitimate and thriving motivation within the social enterprise sector, we suggest that looking to the future in that sector would constitute a large, separate undertaking beyond the scope of this book.

Research choices

The chapters of this book loosely represent the stages of the research process (2012–14) that started with these questions. The introductions provide justification and reflection on our starting point. The Voices section showcases the data we collected. The final sections present our interpretations and thoughts on the meaning of what we have collected.

It is important to note that as researchers and authors we write with a commitment to acknowledging the 'humanness' of all research – that is to say being transparent about the extent to which research is a product of particular people, with previous experience and individual backgrounds, who are deciding to explore areas of interest to them. Rather than suggest that we have somehow emptied ourselves of our preconceptions and claim that our interpretations are exactly the same as any other researchers might have reached given the same data, we offer a different approach.

We invite you to understand our backgrounds and experiences (the personal introductions) and the existing understanding of social enterprises with which we embark on the research process (the introduction chapter) in order to find a different kind of reliability in our work than you might expect from a randomised control trial for a medical experiment. Instead of stressing our objectivity and control of the research situation over all else, we stress our integrity in trying to present a wide variety of different opinions, and our commitment to being open to where each encounter with an interviewee took us. We provide you, the reader, with enough of an understanding of our backgrounds and experience, and of the interviewees' own points of view, to judge whether the interpretations we arrive at in the final sections of this book are the same or different to those you as a reader are taking away with you. From our point of view, if this book stimulates debate about the possible future of social enterprise, it has done its job.

4

The Voices

Changing business

Could social enterprises offer an alternative to mainstream business in the future? This section presents a range of perspectives on the topic of what might be possible.

We kick off this first group of interviews with Sophi Tranchell, who wants us to stop assuming that it is 'natural' that businesses exist to maximise private profit and who reminds us that there are many other ways of doing business that can benefit a broader range of people.

In the next piece, Karin Christiansen highlights how the choice to do business differently can be part of a wider political agenda to promote democracy and mutual self-help.

Roger Spear offers words of caution over the danger of talking up social enterprise as an alternative to both mainstream business and public services without a clear idea of what it can and can't achieve in the current political and economic environment.

Vivian Woodell suggests that people interested in using business to change the world need to be aware of lessons from the history of co-operation but also to engage with what co-operation means in the twenty-first century. They need to be shown what's possible by pioneering and innovative new social enterprises.

Lucy Findlay explains why it's important to define what a social enterprise is and how it is different from mainstream business, in order to help promote the model to a wider audience.

Fergus Lyon also picks up the idea of definition, suggesting that without clarity over what social enterprise means, approaches to social enterprise are coming at the idea of changing business from two different directions at once: one being standardisation as a form of protection against **mission drift** away from social purposes, the other being the greater variety of approaches to providing all types of value through all existing forms of organisation.

SOPHI TRANCHELL
The future needs responsible participation

'It's important to say – there is another way!'

"The future will be as good or bad as we let it be. We as citizens have to participate," insists Sophi Tranchell, managing director at pioneering Fairtrade chocolate company Divine. "People have fought hard for political rights but responsible participation is even more than that, it's about where you buy goods and services and where you work."

For Sophi, social enterprises promote responsible participation by putting a social mission, rather than a purely profit-making mission, at the heart of everything they do. Divine was set up in 1998 to improve the livelihoods of cocoa producers in West Africa – to help them "take home a slice of the value they were helping to create". The Kuapa Kokoo farmers' **co-operative** therefore owns 45 per cent of Divine and is run democratically at the village, district and national level. In this way Divine's example shifts the emphasis within society from 'profit at all costs for a few' to a wider range of advantages for a more diverse set of people. This means that Sophi sees social enterprises as fundamentally different from corporations with well-developed **corporate social responsibility** activities because while some activities might be socially beneficial, the profit-maximising priority at the heart of the business has not been altered.

Yet while Sophi sees social enterprises as promoting responsible participation – by providing examples and giving people alternative places to work and buy – she also recognises that for them to really flourish and become more common in the future, they also need to be supported by a society which provides them with open doors to future development. A wider set of people and organisations need to recognise the need for responsible participation and what it means in practice. For Divine, it means continuing to try to do better: "I don't think doing better is a static thing, we need to continue to raise the bar. We need to concentrate on the value of independent businesses in the face of huge consolidation of food companies in particular. We need to facilitate the coming together of farmers to help them talk about their future and hear their voices. We need to continue to champion traceability and empower consumers to ask these questions." Sophi also hopes, however, that individuals will take on this message of responsible participation and act accordingly.

As an investment for the future, Sophi has been involved in trying to give young people the information they need to make informed choices: "I've been saying, 'You are going to have to work somewhere – but profit-maximisation isn't necessarily going to make you happy'. One of the things that is scary is the image of business portrayed by *Dragon's Den* and *The Apprentice*. It's important to say – there is another way!" Luckily for Sophi, everyone likes to hear about chocolate, "so it's a nice place to start with children and adults". By talking about Divine's mission and successes (including the many mainstream chocolate companies now converting to Fairtrade chocolate in their wake) Sophi is able to talk about things that others in the sector may find it hard to get people interested in: democratic governance, alternative ways of distributing profit, fairness and gender equality. "The co-op that owns us has been impressive in promoting the participation of women – which is particularly impressive in that context – and in 2010 they elected a woman president," explains Sophi, showing how doing business differently goes deeper than just finding different ways to hand out the profits. It's about the people involved and the system they work within: "You need to bring democracy down to more specific things at a more local level – finding a place to have a sensible enough conversation."

Sophi suggests that some of the big changes facing modern society may make people realise the need for this conversation. "It's interesting in the world of chocolate – it's being suggested there won't be enough cocoa to fulfil the forecasted demand. We hear about oil in this context, but forget that it's other resources too," muses Sophi.

"It might be that resources getting more scarce means people have to participate in a more responsible way – to realise for instance that you're throwing away a third of the food you buy now and if you stopped doing that, you could probably afford to pay more for your food." She suggests that an appreciation of scarcity may recalibrate people's assessment of the value of things that they previously saw as cheap or free and therefore took for granted.

Another impetus for change may be that people are slowly becoming aware, after the financial crises that began in 2008, of the immense power and lack of accountability in most corporations, in comparison to governments. "The last five years have been interesting in the sense that people have said capitalism isn't working – it's eating itself." At the same time people have started to realise they do not have sensible ways of holding governments to account over the way they spend people's taxes, for instance around health and social care: "As a person who is ageing, I start to think, there must be more exciting ways to do elderly care. There's been a strange thing happened where accountability has been divorced from the democratic process as it stands. They're running the care on your behalf but is it running in a way you'd be happy with – if not what can you do about it?"

For Sophi it's important for people to realise that the obsession with maximising private profit is "not natural", it's just one way of doing business. Ultimately, in our purchasing and employment decisions she thinks that social enterprises could give us the opportunity to explore other ways of doing business, ways which tackle rather than reinforce inequality. She wonders if people in the future will start to examine "who they are actually working to create value for. If it's for someone else – why should only company owners or shareholders benefit rather than the value being shared collectively? Wouldn't that make more sense?"

About Sophi Tranchell MBE

Sophi is managing director of Divine Chocolate Ltd, the innovative Fairtrade company co-owned by cocoa farmers. Previously she worked for the Metro Tartan art cinema group, introducing top foreign films to big new UK audiences. Both in her personal and work life, Sophi has, from a young age, been active in supporting social justice, leading her also to be very curious about who owns whom in the business world.

As well as growing a popular Fairtrade chocolate brand in a highly competitive market, for 13 years she has campaigned energetically for the terms of trade for small-scale producers to change, and promoted more socially responsible business models. Sophi has been an elected director and co-chair of Social Enterprise London and, as chair of the Fairtrade London steering committee, she successfully led the campaign to 'Make London a Fairtrade City'. In 2010 she was given a Social Entrepreneur Award of the Year by Ernst & Young, and in 2013 she was awarded a Good Deals Pioneer Award for leading social entrepreneurs. In the New Year's Honours List 2008/09 Sophi was made an MBE for services to the food industry, and is on the London Food Board led by Rosie Boycott.

About Divine

Divine Chocolate is the only mainstream chocolate company 45 per cent owned by the farmers in Ghana who supply its cocoa – so they share Divine profits as well as receiving the Fairtrade price for their cocoa. Back in 1997 the Kuapa Kokoo cocoa farmers' co-operative voted at their AGM to set up a chocolate company in order to access the valuable chocolate market and a year later the first Divine bar was launched in the UK. The company was established with the aim 'to improve the livelihood of smallholder cocoa producers in West Africa by establishing their own dynamic branded proposition in the UK chocolate market, thus putting them higher up the value chain'. This mission continues to drive the company's development – and to this end they have successfully both grown sales, and been at the forefront of raising consumer, business and government awareness about the need for fairer trade as well as the catalyst for change in the industry. Divine is also growing its business in the USA, and is available across most of Europe.

Kuapa Kokoo receives four streams of income from Divine Chocolate – the price of the cocoa, the Fairtrade premium ($200 on every tonne), a producer support and development (PS&D) fund (2 per cent of turnover) and 45 per cent of distributable profit. Kuapa Kokoo distributes a bonus from the Fairtrade premium and invests it in improving living conditions, education opportunities, healthcare and sanitation for its members – projects voted for by its members. The PS&D money goes towards maintaining the democratic process and most recently towards an innovative Kuapa radio broadcast. The Dividend is invested in key materials for members and into Kuapa Kokoo's business.

Kuapa Kokoo's ownership of Divine Chocolate is delivering profits, knowledge and power to farmers – and they also have a pride in ensuring they produce the 'best of the best' cocoa for their own chocolate company: www.divinechocolate.com

KARIN CHRISTIANSEN
Social enterprise as part of a wider political framework

'Human beings can do great things together.'

Karin Christiansen has been general secretary of the Co-operative Party since 2012 and her thoughts about the future of social enterprise come from the perspective of a movement that started in the 1840s. But first, we have to clarify the difference between social enterprises and co-operatives. Karin is aware that for some people this is a heavily loaded question, "In part it's a fascinating conceptual debate," she says, "but in part it's dancing on the head of a pin." Karin makes light of the differences, "The co-op movement and the social enterprise movement come from the same place – people using business and enterprise to change their circumstances. Some co-ops are social enterprises and some social enterprises are co-ops." Ultimately these are enterprises that are not just concerned with profits and which "often empower the users of these services or goods".

The co-operative movement perhaps shows the way forward for its baby sister, social enterprise. As well as its large-scale businesses and financial institutions, it also has a party political identity, working jointly with the Labour Party, with which it has a "huge ideological, historical relationship". Democracy is a key principle within co-ops and something that perhaps the social enterprise sector could learn more about from the extensive experience of the co-op movement. "We have a solid theory of democracy," Karin reminds me, "it's not just an ethical thing but it is important who runs a business and who profits from it."

"In the nineteenth century, co-ops changed the way retail organisations operated, developing new standards in food [production and selling]. We need to influence the norms in today's markets." The **Rochdale Pioneers** who set up the first retail co-op in 1844, did so mostly so that they and their community could buy unadulterated food in the context of the urbanisation that followed the industrial revolution. Karin sees parallels with the way that the social enterprise sector could influence the economy in future. Currently, she says, the problem is the "precedence of the shareholder model of business that is only concerned with profit making. Once they have made their profits, any way they can, we have to regulate and tax them. They cause damage and society has to mitigate it. Businesses should have wider social objectives wired into their purpose – a form of 'pre-distribution' so that we don't have to correct problems after the fact."

Karin says that there is nothing wrong with markets, "they're just a tool for exchange, but we should be asking more questions about how they operate".

"Human self-interest is social. If there are people hungry on the streets where I live it makes me feel terrible. If they're not there, I feel better, so a more equal society is better for everyone."

Karin thinks that one way social enterprises will exert their influence in future is by taking on more public services. She thinks that the boundaries between public and private sectors are already blurred and will continue to be less distinctive. Public service mutual models are important. Foundation trusts, set up in the NHS under the previous Labour government "partly worked, but there wasn't enough patient involvement. The co-op movement has a lot to teach about how you get better at public services and how to engage people." But this is not without risks. "There are huge risks with **public service mutuals**; there are potential benefits but are they genuine enterprises and not just sub-contracting entities?" She thinks that co-ops can be part of this change and should be pragmatic about it. In fact she describes this as "joyful pragmatism; if there's a problem, let's solve it". Significantly, she also says, "I reject the idea that co-ops can't be scaled up. We're not just small and cute, we can scale up."

As people have begun to question the roles of business and finance in society, Karin describes how this presents a great opportunity for co-ops and social enterprises in future. "The movement needs to step up and take on these challenges, we must be brave and innovative, we need to support each other and to have the confidence to do that." But she also recognises that there can be problems with the information that is given to people about co-ops and social enterprises and that this can sometimes be confusing.

"We make it hard for people to understand us sometimes. We pick at the finer points and the differences between us rather than focusing on what we have in common. We need to be more realistic about what people understand about us – and the starting point should be them not us. We need to find better ways of explaining what we do and why it matters."

Karin says that what is unique about the co-op movement is that it has a history of 150 years of radicalism and that throughout this time its ideas and methods have been thoroughly tested. This puts the co-op sector in a good position to challenge the cynicism and apathy that pervades political life in the early twenty-first century. "The Rochdale Pioneers were the original community organisers. Today we need to get good people into politics, to be a place for people who want to change the world. It's not simple but we have to contribute to overcoming cynicism about the political realm or we're in serious trouble. We have a responsibility to step up."

This can start in the co-operative movement, where, she thinks, not enough of its members know that they are members and what that entails, "We need a higher percentage converting from just having a [co-op member's] card to doing something about it." She thinks that the co-operative values of solidarity, equity and social justice will continue to resonate with people but that some people have valid concerns about what this way of working will involve. After all, she concedes "No one wants to work in a collective where no one does the washing up. We've got ways of dealing with these issues and we mustn't forget them, because we can be big and powerful."

About Karin Christiansen

Karin has been general secretary of the Co-operative Party since September 2012.

Karin's long career in international development includes her role as the founder and director of Publish What You Fund, the global campaign for aid transparency. Prior to that she was the European policy manager with the ONE Campaign and for many years was a research fellow at the Overseas Development Institute. She joined ODI having worked as an economist at the Rwandan Ministry of Finance and the Ministry of Agriculture. Prior to that Karin worked for the United Nations High Commissioner for Refugees in Croatia. She has master's degrees in development economics and in social and political thought.

In 2011 Karin was named as one of the Devex London 2011 40 Under 40 International Development Leaders. She is a board member of Maslaha and Publish What You Fund. Karin was also one of the founders the UK think tank transparency website, Who Funds You?, and of Labour Values.

ROGER SPEAR

Social enterprise keeps the private sector honest and the public sector accountable

'Now is the time to turn rhetoric into reality.'

There is a clear and influential role for social enterprises in a changing economic environment according to Professor Roger Spear, who has been researching and writing about social enterprises for over 20 years. Roger thinks that social enterprises are part of a wider movement of social benefit in the economy, that there are lots of different ways of doing this but social enterprise is at the core. He describes this flexible and changing picture as one of "diversity and hybridity" but thinks that within this fluidity it is vital to have fixed eligibility criteria to be a social enterprise so that the integrity of the sector is protected.

"Social enterprise is social enterprise," he told me, "but other operators, such as the more entrepreneurial parts of the public sector and socially aware sections of the private sector circulate around it." Roger is one of the founders of EMES, the European social enterprise research network, and much of his work has been studying the international co-operative and social enterprise movements. He sees the UK social enterprise sector as being influenced from two directions: from mainland Europe the focus is on building social capital and seeking social change; while from the United States there is a growing culture of social entrepreneurship. Roger identifies diverse origins for emerging social enterprises, for instance greater income generation through trading by charities, the conversion of existing businesses into co-operative or employee-owned forms and the externalisation of public services. These types of changes can be seen as hybridisation of more traditional organisational forms. The result is different ways of working and engaging with the community, but Roger admits, "I'm worried that as Marx might have said, the social enterprise sector becomes a dwarfish form, and legitimises a form of back door privatisation of the public sector." One form of hybrid comes from the changing world of public services – but Roger suggests that whatever form they take we will find that these heavily regulated forms of externalised public services are similar to genuine social enterprises, as regulation reduces diversity. This is a conscious move by governments. The coalition government, according to Roger, is "attempting to replicate famous models such as John Lewis without real understanding of the structure and how it contributes to the success of the business".

Yet a benefit of this process will be the increased level of user involvement in public services such as health, leading to another hybrid. "People will be taking more responsibility for their own health and participating in planning their healthcare. This doesn't necessarily make it a social enterprise but it's part of the spectrum. In heavily regulated sectors such as elder care, it may be difficult to tell the difference."

Other forms that interest Roger are the organisations set up by social entrepreneurs. He thinks that these can be led by individuals who are driven by a mixture of "religious revivalism and the desire to change the world". He describes them as "naïve but potentially inspiring individuals. They're not always rooted in reality but sometimes their energy and enthusiasm can be infectious and they do get things done. They are most visible in the US-led international activities such as the Skoll Foundation, but also within some home-grown organisations such as the School for Social Entrepreneurs and UnLtd."

Within this context of hybridity and diversity, Roger thinks that it is critical that there is certification of social enterprise, even though "it is heavily politically contested". If social enterprises want to claim leadership of this movement and to make sure it is not hijacked by others with different motives, the core criteria of social enterprises must be fixed and protected, as a beacon of value-based practices.

Roger talks in detail about the opportunities and threats for social enterprises in the context of delivering public services. The biggest concern, he thinks, is the size of contracts that are being put out to tender. "In long periods of austerity, the size and economies of scale of contracts will become more important – and this favours large, for-profit organisations." This has led to a sub-contracting role for social enterprises. Roger thinks that the other players will be less recognised forms of social enterprise "supercharities, the big brand names that are growing and being more successful", but he wonders if "they will grow more like big business or will they sustain their community and social values as they grow".

Roger is concerned that there are dangers for the social enterprise sector, of a "crashing wave of built-up expectation", if some of the results that have been promised are not realised. Roger thinks that some significant failures including the demutualisation of building societies in the 1990s and the emergency refinancing of the Co-operative Bank (which took place during the week of our interview), may have caused lasting damage to the credibility of the sector. But even if there are financial and economic failures, it will be important to be able to point to ethical businesses with good ethical practice.

At the time of this interview, Roger was taking part in a research study, mapping social enterprises in all 29 member states of the European Union. He says there is a marked difference between the views of "old Europe – the first 15 members, that operate in the context of the social economy," with those of the newer members, from Eastern Europe where there is more interest in the enterprise part of social enterprise. He says that some of his European colleagues see the UK as being "halfway across the Atlantic".

For the future, Roger thinks that it is important that there are now degree courses in social enterprise and a significant research base, but he is concerned that some research organisations are biased towards the traditional voluntary sector approach and are unduly cautious and critical of social enterprise.

In Roger's opinion, the biggest challenge for social enterprises is to manage their relationship with the media, to have more influence over public perceptions. "I'd like the general public to be more concerned about the potential for improving citizenship and the other benefits of the social enterprise sector. It's important for ordinary people to understand the role of social enterprise. However, in order for this to happen, "I think it is important that all the voices in the social enterprise space, the traditional voluntary sector, co-ops and **mutuals** and the different membership organisations and umbrella bodies, stop playing identity games in this contested policy environment." Overall, he concludes, there has been a positive narrative about social enterprise, "but now is the time to turn that rhetoric into reality".

About Professor Roger Spear

Roger Spear is Professor of Social Entrepreneurship and chair of the Co-operatives Research Unit, member of the Ciriec Scientific Committee, founder member and vice-president of the EMES research network on social enterprise, and teaches organisational systems and research methods in the Department of Communication and Systems at the Open University.

He is widely known for research on innovation and development in the **third sector**, particularly social enterprises. Studies have included a study of labour market work integration in several European countries, and a comparative study of social enterprises in Europe. Recent projects include: being part of a team evaluating the UK government's social enterprise strategy (with GHK); two UNDP-funded projects on social enterprise in Eastern Europe and former CIS countries; and a much-quoted research project on governance and social enterprise.

He has been an expert consultant on several OECD projects on the social economy in Korea, Slovenia, and Serbia. He is also currently guest professor at Roskilde University, Copenhagen, Denmark, where he helped coordinate a GEM study of social entrepreneurship, and contributes to a pioneering International Masters in Social Entrepreneurship.

VIVIAN WOODELL
Showing what is possible

'The co-op movement as a whole has gone from being a sleepy thing to thinking it can be a force in the world.'

Vivian Woodell is the chief executive of The Phone Co-op and has an enviable pedigree of involvement with co-operatives dating back to the 1980s. So when I ask him to imagine the future, it turns out that in terms of redefining the co-operative movement, he's been there, done that, and has some useful pointers to share.

"It was 1983, soon after I left university and I'd joined the Labour Party, so I started shopping at the co-op – I thought it could be important but I didn't really know how," Vivian explains. Prompted by a friend from Ghana, he started to wonder why the co-op was still selling South African goods, at a time when boycotts on political grounds were common. After receiving an unsatisfactory brush-off to his letter of enquiry, he remembers thinking "I'm a member of this thing, I should be able to propose a motion." So, Vivian's journey into exploring the world of co-operatives began. "I was fascinated by the fact that there was a business of this scale owned by members (ordinary people), not city investors."

Although there have been recent adverts highlighting the values that underpin the Co-operative brand and even an International Year of Co-operatives in 2012, in the 1980s, Vivian suggests that the social means and ends of co-operation were slipping into the background. "We felt it needed to rediscover its purpose, rediscover the aims of the movement's founders, remember the **Rochdale principles** and see what that way of thinking would look like in a modern context," he tells me. "That's how I got involved. It was a group of us agitating and asking questions. We started to press for change."

So when Vivian and others started asking what co-operation meant in the late twentieth century, they started to think about who the business was serving and why. The early co-operatives were about working from a value-base to serve the most basic human needs (for instance affordable, untainted food). Different economic times could mean applying that same value-base to fulfilling a far wider range of issues. "It was about marketing our co-operative advantage. We produced model stores in which values were central to the business – concept stores if you like. Elements of what was started there have found their way into [the stores you see today]."

We see, then, that co-operatives have already been re-imagined: "The co-op movement as a whole has gone from being a kind of sleepy thing to thinking it can be a force in the world – people rediscovering ways of managing that can reflect their values." So, the question has to be, what is there to do in the twenty-first century? Vivian sees the future in a wide range of different sectors and activities: "The Rochdale pioneers started food shops because that was the need. So where are the areas where the state and private business aren't providing now?"

In the same vein, Vivian is keen that the co-operative movement does not lose its reputation for innovation. Referring to The Phone Co-op, he defines the type of innovation he means: "We don't take big risks on technology that needs investment as we don't think that's a good way to use our members' share capital – we're not innovators in the technical sense, but we're innovators in a social and economic sense."

Yet, Vivian's own early story highlights one of the issues which the co-operative movement faces. He started to shop at co-ops without quite knowing why it was important, even if he soon moved beyond that lack of understanding. As we discuss the future, lack of understanding seems to be one potential barrier to further growth of co-operation: "I don't think there's enough public awareness of what co-ops can do," suggests Vivian. "I think we've got much more to do…"

One sign of progress would be to see more consumer co-ops being established – "a consumer co-op movement not afraid to go into new things," suggests Vivian. He traces his motivation for being part of starting a new consumer co-op in the difficult area of telecoms, not just to a recognition of a need (lower phone bills for **non-governmental organisations** making international calls), but also to a determination to show it could work: "What motivated me…was the desire to be taken seriously" by those in existing co-operative businesses who had allowed the movement to move away from its value-base because they thought that values got in the way of the business. Given the success of the Phone Co-op now, with 23,000 customers, and 10,000 members and a turnover in 2013 of £10.6 million, it's perhaps hard to imagine that there were people who thought it couldn't be done: "I wanted to show that you could do it differently, show that people who had this kind of idea weren't just impractical idealists – we could return a profit and run a business."

Well into the start of the twenty-first century, The Phone Co-op is flourishing and that original intent is still driving its success. But Vivian suggests we aren't seeing many new consumer co-ops outside of certain specialist sectors and this must partly be down to awareness and partly to motivation: "Where does the entrepreneurial drive to do that come from?" Vivian asks, "A group of people need the idea, the will to do it and they need to know what's possible."

One way of fostering entrepreneurial drive could be through example, showing the possibilities that open up if people have a new awareness of who business is actually serving. "The Co-operative Commission report *The co-operative advantage* (2001) defined the purpose of the co-operative movement to challenge traditional UK business with an alternative, better model for business and the economy," Vivian explains. It's an ambitious aim, but he suggests that The Phone Co-op is serving as an example of how it could be achieved: "You can run a business differently in this kind of industry." The message to take away is – 'It is possible.'

About Vivian Woodell

Vivian Woodell is the founder and chief executive of The Phone Co-op, the UK's only telecommunications provider which is 100 per cent owned by its customers. Since it was set up in 1998, The Phone Co-op has built a profitable business with 23,000 residential and business customers, over 60 employees, and an annual turnover of £10 million at the time of writing in 2013.

Vivian is also an elected director of The Midcounties Co-operative, one of the UK's largest independent retail co-operatives, where he served as president for eight years, and a director of Co-operatives UK, the national trade body for co-operatives.

Prior to starting The Phone Co-op, Vivian had worked extensively in the co-operative movement. His earlier roles include: executive director of the Social Economy Consortium, which managed Co-operative and Social Economy development projects in Central and Eastern Europe, and project manager with the European Social Economy Information Network, ARIES. In the past he has served as a board member of the European Confederation of Workers' Cooperatives, Social Cooperatives and Social and Participative Enterprises (CECOP) and a member of the executive of the International Organisation of Industrial, Artisanal and Service Producers' Co-operatives, CICOPA.

About The Phone Co-op

The Phone Co-op is an independent consumer co-operative based in Manchester, Chipping Norton and London. It is the only telecoms provider in the UK that is 100 per cent owned by its customers.

The Phone Co-op operates nationwide, providing fixed and mobile telecommunications services to over 23,000 residential and business customers, including other co-operatives, charities and third sector organisations. In fact, it was set up in 1998 to provide telecommunications services to charities and fellow co-operatives by allowing them to purchase collectively. The Phone Co-op has grown every year since then and, in 2012, it adopted the nationally recognised Co-operative brand and started trading as The Co-operative Phone and Broadband, The Co-operative Mobile, and The Co-operative Business Telecoms to reflect the range of services it provides.

As a consumer co-operative, The Phone Co-op is owned by its customers who can influence how the organisation is run. By electing its directors and attending its AGM, all its members can have an equal say in the decisions The Phone Co-op makes. Members also participate in its business success and receive a share of profits – this is paid in the form of a dividend which is distributed among members according to what they spend with the co-operative. This dividend reached 2.5 per cent of sales to members in 2013.

Because it is owned by its customers, The Phone Co-op puts people at the centre of everything it does. It is committed to offering the best possible service and to operating with honesty, openness and a sense of social responsibility, caring for its customers, its staff, its communities and the planet. For customers, this translates into fair and transparent pricing with no hidden charges.

The Phone Co-op is also a fair employer. In 2012, it was accredited as a Living Wage Employer, and it has an Employee Council and encourages trade union membership.

The Phone Co-op is also committed to providing greener telecoms by guaranteeing energy efficiency in its offices, using electricity from renewable sources and offsetting all the carbon dioxide that it and its telecoms suppliers generate, reducing its paper usage and using recycled paper and stationery. This co-operative also promotes the use of public transport by staff and visitors, and offers bicycles to employees.

Mainly through its Co-operative and Social Economy Development Fund, which was set up to help community-owned projects, The Phone Co-op invests in initiatives that make a difference locally and globally. This includes not only renewable energy but also community projects. Up to 2013, The Phone Co-op had allocated over £324,000 to that fund.

After 15 years of trading, The Phone Co-op is proving that it is possible to run a successful business while behaving ethically and with a sense of social responsibility.

LUCY FINDLAY

Social enterprises: the business of choice

'How can you argue it's a good thing if you don't know a particular organisation actually is a social enterprise?'

Lucy Findlay's vision for the future is that social enterprises become the businesses of choice for us all. Her business is to make sure that we all know what they are and what they do so that we can buy from them while contributing to their social and environmental goals.

Lucy is the managing director of the Social Enterprise Mark (SEM) CIC, which runs the nationally recognised certification for social enterprises. She thinks that the social enterprise sector has become too caught up in a technical debate about what social enterprises are and that this has made it too difficult for members of the public and others to understand what the difference is between social enterprises and other business models. The SEM has worked out eligibility criteria so that Lucy's definition of social enterprise is very clear.

"Social enterprises have to be trading for social or environmental aims and objectives and this has to be written into their constitution; they must distribute no more than 50 per cent of their profits to shareholders; there must be an **asset lock** and/or distribution clause protecting the resources owned by the business in favour of its aims; they must earn 50 per cent of their income through trading and they must have had some form of external validation to prove that they are meeting their aims and objectives." The SEM is adding criteria about employee engagement currently and will also further develop criteria around social and environmental impact.

Lucy's view is that having clear criteria in place to define social enterprises is very important. "We need to get across that organisations are doing great stuff," she says. "It is a complex message to get across to the public, which is why we need the Mark to put across a simple message without others – including the customer – having to understand everything that sits behind it."

She comes across a lot of confusion among policy makers and influencers. "I don't understand how people can lobby for social enterprises without having a common fundamental understanding of what they are. This blurriness is happening at all levels, which leads to many misunderstandings. Intellectually it's a real problem; how can you argue that it's a good thing if you don't know a particular organisation actually is a social enterprise? It seems that, currently, any business can call itself one without legitimate challenge. Many people say it doesn't matter, only the impact matters, not what you call them. However, this could result in those who are primarily concerned with shareholder profit 'piggy backing' on the values of social enterprise without buying into those values. It also potentially taints fundamental understanding of social enterprises, for example as in the current debate about social enterprise being 'privatisation by the backdoor' where public services are being externalised."

This is why Lucy thinks the Mark is so important. It is acting as an incentive for people to become bona fide social enterprises. "Evidence from our registrations shows that a significant but small minority are not eligible, " she says, "However, just by registering they are showing that they think that they might be eligible. In many cases this stimulates them to find out what they can do to become eligible, increasing the robustness of the social enterprise population as a whole and ensuring that certification can provide reassurance. Trends are showing that we are dealing with a growing number of traditional businesses that want to convert into social enterprises."

Lucy's view is that things are changing on various fronts. Her work with big corporates in the City of London has been revealing. "One of the big banks said that if social enterprises are to become part of their supply chain then they need to be clear that they are the genuine article." It also helps to find them (a perennial problem). Opening up markets is one way of developing social enterprises, another is to spread the word. One particular audience is receptive to this model of doing business. "Young people really get it and they want to go for it."

Lucy's vision for the future is that there are more genuine social enterprises delivering in all sectors of the economy, especially where gaps currently exist. She thinks that people in the social enterprise sector have got too hung up on delivering public services but says that there is real potential elsewhere. "There are great opportunities for lawyers' practices and the professions generally. Wouldn't it be great if the huge profits made by these professions were re-invested for social and environmental benefit? I don't see why not."

She says that we have a business model that is based on international capitalism but that it needn't be the only one. The social enterprise model prioritises tackling social and environmental issues, not just wealth creation. As more people become more aware that life isn't just about the next fast car, there is a real opportunity for social enterprises to make a difference. "Business profits can be used to tackle the big issues in the world, it could lead to us behaving in a less individualistic way and contribute to social and environmental justice."

About Lucy Findlay

Lucy Findlay is the founding managing director of the Social Enterprise Mark CIC. The Social Enterprise Mark is the only certification for genuine social enterprises. The Mark is the first development of its kind in the social enterprise world. In 2013 there were more than 450 Mark holders throughout the UK and it was attracting international attention.

Lucy was formerly the chief executive of RISE, the South West regional network for social enterprises, which founded the Social Enterprise Mark and developed innovative approaches in the specialist business support arena.

In her work she has advised a number of government ministers and departments including CLG, BIS, DEFRA and the Cabinet Office, but her key passion is working with social enterprises to ensure that they are recognised as a legitimate and different way of doing business. Originally training as a town planner, she found that she was far more interested in people and started her career in community regeneration and policy for the Development Trusts Association (Locality) and ACRE. She also got a feel for the civil service by working on secondment for a number of years. She has been a director on a number of boards including Social Enterprise UK and is a fellow of the RSA.

About the Social Enterprise Mark

The Social Enterprise Mark CIC is the only certification authority for social enterprises.

Social enterprises have to prove that they are genuine against a set of qualification criteria, which is overseen by an independent Certification Panel to ensure fairness and consistency.

As a catalyst for social and environmental change, the Mark is bringing social enterprises together to be advocates for a bigger, better society. Proud to be part of a movement, putting people and planet at the very heart of the bottom line, they celebrate the solutions that social enterprises are delivering in society today.

Consumers will recognise that businesses displaying the Mark are trading to benefit people and the planet, and businesses will be assured that by buying from certified social enterprises, they protect their own credibility through corporate responsibility and the 50in250 campaign.

The Social Enterprise Mark aims to communicate the ethical values represented by social enterprises to a range of audiences, emphasising the principle that social enterprises are businesses trading for people and planet, not private profit.

The Social Enterprise Mark operates as a **Community Interest Company** (CIC) limited by shares. A steering group made up of social enterprise leaders and supporters agreed that a Mark was important for the sector and together agreed its design, purpose and criteria. It was informed by the Social Enterprise Mark already piloted by Rise in the South West of England.

FERGUS LYON
Keeping an eye on the trends as they develop

'Because the idea of social value is so personal and it's based on values and views, having a common currency is difficult.'

As an established researcher on the topic of social enterprises and entrepreneurship, Professor Fergus Lyon has been keeping an eye on trends in the sector for a while now. "As a researcher, I'm interested in how concepts are emerging and how they are used for different purposes," he explains. He sees his role as that of an objective observer and shares his reflections with us. He uses a broad definition of social enterprise that encompasses any "organisations that are trading with a social purpose". For Fergus, it is this social purpose that is the key to understanding and defining what a social enterprise is: "The distinction is its primary social purpose." He contrasts the primary social purpose of a social enterprise with the many positive social outcomes that private businesses can and do have while they are pursuing their primary purpose: profit for their owners. "If you think about employment, apprenticeships, tackling unemployment, social services like providing care, health services – these all have huge benefits for the country," Fergus suggests, but reminds us that these benefits are not the stated primary reason why these companies exist.

While he is happy to use a broad definition, he suggests that the lack of a *clear* definition that is accepted by everyone involved in the sector, however broad it may be, may be a problem for the future of social enterprises. He suggests that those promoting social enterprise are pushing the sector in two different directions, with some proponents seeming to press for both at once. The first direction is towards a tighter definition of social enterprise involving features like an asset lock and set of written criteria for judging the legitimacy of an organisation calling itself a social enterprise. He suggests the Social Enterprise Mark is an example of this direction. The second direction is towards what some people have called 'social purpose businesses' where there is less of a concern about building social mechanisms into the structure of the model and more of a focus on delivering outcomes in whatever way works best. He thinks the latter could deliver "more conventional services, but may miss out on some of the specifically social features of social enterprise like engagement [of workers, consumers or the local community]. But the scale of this type of social business could have a big impact."

So the issue as Fergus defines it, is that "at the moment [social enterprise] is trying to do both. With that vagueness there's always going to be space for so-called social enterprises getting into the media that do cheat and that profiteer from social purpose – which would be unacceptable for the social enterprise sector." Although he suggests that there are always going to be those who bend the rules and abuse models that are supposed to be for the public good – the danger of this for the social enterprise sector is greater than for established models like charities. In the case of the established and well-known idea of a charity, any abuse of the system can be blamed on the faults of the people involved rather than the model. However, for a still largely unknown model like social enterprise, Fergus wonders whether any scandals could end up being attributed to the social enterprise model itself.

As well as abuses of the term, Fergus suggests that a clear constraint to the mainstreaming of social enterprise is lack of awareness: "there aren't high street examples or flagship social enterprises in local communities". However, he suggests that there are now social enterprises run by people who otherwise might have gone into the private sector – as a result of interest from those who want their start-ups to do something different from traditional businesses. The problem of getting across the message of these new start-ups, says Fergus, is that it's a hard concept to convey to potential customers: "Saying that we've got a social purpose and it's not for personal benefit is hard to show." This is because we have not yet determined to everyone's satisfaction how to define or place value on social outcomes. "If you are having it [social purpose] as your core reason, you've got to have a clear way of determining if it's happening. Because the idea of social value is so personal and it's based on values and views, having a common currency is difficult."

This idea of finding a common currency to determine whether organisations are providing social outcomes is of particular relevance when it comes to public service **commissioning**. After all, commissioners and **procurement** officers have to base their decisions on some kind of information about the tenders they are assessing. While in the past these decisions may have been made on financial stability or output targets, "this should change with outcome-based commissioning. They can be more innovative in determining those [assessment criteria]." However, "you need a high quality of commissioners willing to take the risks involved," says Fergus. While the **Social Value Act 2012** provides 'something down on paper' to legitimise these decisions, it does not mean that it is happening everywhere.

Fergus is concerned about another aspect of these developments, "There are now some social enterprises that are completely reliant on public sector contracts – does that mean that they have been co-opted by the state? That's the question," he muses, exploring some of the critical thinking on social enterprises and their involvement with government. There are some who would say that it wouldn't matter if they had, as long as they were providing the outcomes, and others who stick to the idea that the social purpose of a social enterprise is not just in what it does, but how it does it.

Fergus has no intention of pushing a particular definition and does not want to see others getting obsessed with defining social enterprises either, but his concern is that in 20 years' time, if the concept of social enterprise is still "muddling along in the middle" it won't "take hold in the public imagination". So even if there are organisations around that look like the organisations we call social enterprises today – Fergus suggests that lack of clarity now will lead to extinction of the term 'social enterprise' in the future. He suggests that if this confusion is not addressed, another term will emerge and enter into common use and the term social enterprise will have been just another trend.

About Fergus Lyon

Fergus Lyon is Professor of Enterprise and Organisations in the Centre for Enterprise and Economic Development Research, Middlesex University, with a specialisation in social enterprises. He directs research programmes on social enterprise, investment, innovation, enterprise development and related public policy as well as being an associate director (social enterprise lead) of the ESRC Third Sector Research Centre and director of the ESRC Social Enterprise Capacity Building Cluster. He has over 20 years of experience researching and advising on social enterprises.

In 2007 he was seconded to the Prime Minister's Strategy Unit in the Cabinet Office. He is also a founder and director of a social enterprise preschool. He is on the editorial board of the *Social Enterprise Journal*. Fergus has over 120 publications including 30 papers in established international journals, 20 book chapters, a number of shorter policy briefings and two books on social research methodologies.

Different ways to grow

While many interviewees want social enterprise approaches to become more common and the sector to grow, these pieces remind us that there is more than one way to grow and more than one reason for wanting to do so.

Social enterprise approaches are only going to change mainstream ways of doing business, Peter Ramsden argues, if they reach a critical mass in the marketplace.

Matt Stevenson-Dodd reminds us that it's more important for social enterprises to be responsive to trends and changes in the market in which they operate, than to forge ahead, fixed on growth without an eye to sustainability.

Jenny Sims highlights that it can be prudent to grow slowly to keep social enterprises in touch with their social mission. This involves keeping democratic and purposeful contact with the people the social enterprise is set up to support.

Iain Tuckett shows how social enterprises have the option of expanding the range of businesses they operate within an area, for the good of the people in that area.

Shaun Doran favours many different types of growth for different social enterprises, but suggests that some could grow very large indeed if only social enterprises could recognise the key barriers that are holding them back.

PETER RAMSDEN
Reaching critical mass

'I'm not just interested in numbers, I'm interested in quality too.
But you do need the numbers.'

Peter Ramsden would like to see the social enterprise sector growing and influencing mainstream business over the next 20 years. He would like to – but he thinks we are a long way from that possibility. "My fear is that it'll be roughly where it is now," Peter says. "The sector has had enormous support in the last ten years and it hasn't really moved on. At the current rate of progress we will see growth but not a transformative expansion."

Peter can think of a number of ways of helping the sector along. "There's not been enough attention paid to markets," he says, talking about both the closed nature of public service markets which are dominated by huge companies, but also the ability within social enterprises to find a sustainable source of income. "There's been a fragmentation of support…with most business support designed for people and businesses that don't need it," he says. Additionally, he suggests the availability of appropriate finance continues to be a problem that will not be solved just by transitioning from start-up grants with loans for capital and growth: "New funds such as those from Big Society Capital are mostly lending to safe and proven borrowers including the enterprise arms of major charities and for borrowing secured against property."

According to Peter, undeveloped markets, inappropriate support and lack of finance all contribute to a lack of progress for the sector. As we discuss how to overcome these different, wide-ranging barriers, one idea starts to come through strongly. While we can talk all we like about helping individuals to start organisations ("I've got quite a firm view that coaching is the best form of support") and about the oddness of UK local authorities being much worse than the French at building **social clauses** into commissioning, eventually discussion keeps returning to the issue of scale. To put it bluntly: "I think size matters," says Peter.

"A lot of people are running lifestyle social businesses and that's fine, for what it is. But we have so many examples of micro-enterprises," he explains. The issue with this is that if one very successful social enterprise can help, say, 20 young people at once, it's not making a significant or nationally visible difference to the overall situation of young people in the country. Yet, without that significant difference, how is awareness of social enterprise possibilities ever going to be realised in a wider public? "I think awareness would most likely come from specific brands that make it part of their model and promote it as part of their brand." He suggests that only a larger-scale social enterprise would be able to make that breakthrough, in the same ways as say, fair trade.

I put it to Peter that he seems to be suggesting social enterprise will have to reach a critical mass before it becomes part of the everyday. Yet to an extent, waiting for a critical mass of social enterprises to create awareness, so that there can be more social enterprises and more awareness, is an almost chicken and egg style situation. So I ask, what can be done to break out of that circular argument?"We need a programme to help medium-sized social enterprises grow and replicate and carry on delivering social value. You need a different strategy from replicating medium and large enterprises to supporting start-up. I don't think there's been enough of that," Peter suggests. "I'm not just interested in numbers, I'm interested in quality too. But you do need the numbers." He talks both about growth, which is common in business, but also about replication. If the small size of the organisation is a bonus, why not just have lots of them? "Sometimes there's a local reaction against allowing these organisations to spread." Peter tells me about a number of areas where local authorities have tried to set up their own new models (for example in construction apprenticeships) rather than listening to the advice of existing social enterprises and franchising across: "The local authorities must recognise that social enterprises have the experience. They should be prepared to open their market and encourage a successful model from another area to come to their city."

Peter suggests that we need not just to make support available to social enterprises, but to look to them in their turn for support and insight too: "The best way of organising these things is through people who've already done it. Experienced social entrepreneurs would be the best coaches."

There's also another way to foster critical mass – and it's a route that is new and emerging. "Business schools are very important," according to Peter. "There are people now who got into social enterprise because there was a unit on it in their MBA." This normalisation of social enterprise through the education system is one way of switching business-minded people on to the possibilities of creating wide-ranging business contributions to society.

Peter thinks that there will be a lot for these new business people to do: "We are facing massive challenges – we need both business and public services to be providing safe, secure and transparent products whether in healthcare or financial services." Given what Peter sees as the decline in the **post-war social contract**, there are many ways that "social enterprises can enable people's quality of life to become more secure – for instance in the support economy by improving the cost and quality of child [care] or elder care." He suggests that in the face of declining welfare and unstable labour markets, social enterprises could make a difference.

However, as a parting shot, Peter suggests that the social enterprise sector is not the whole answer: "It's unlikely that social enterprises will be able to do this themselves. They'll need partnerships with the private and public sectors – partnerships with social innovation at the heart of them." For this reason he thinks that there is a strong role for the public sector to play in facilitating a more hybrid value-based economy.

About Peter Ramsden

Peter Ramsden is managing director of Freiss Ltd, a small consultancy with an interest in innovation and change. At the time of writing he was involved in a European project sharing knowledge on sustainable urban development. His previous work included positions at The Centre for Economic and Social Inclusion and The New Economics Foundation and before that he was engaged in neighbourhood and community work.

MATT STEVENSON-DODD
Excellence in many niches

'There aren't enough social enterprise leaders already. It's about
how to bring in the talent.'

For Matt Stevenson-Dodd, of youth football charity Street League,
successful social enterprise is "all about state of mind". He's
passionate about leadership and through his work as a youth leader,
MBA graduate and social entrepreneur he's amassed an interesting
combination of hard-nosed business sense and a solid set of core
social values that he'd like to see combined more often in the social
enterprise sector in the future. "There aren't enough social enterprise
leaders already. It's about how to bring in the talent."

For Matt, this isn't only about parachuting in skills from the
business world. "I've seen guys from the private sector trying to
move into charities and they don't get anywhere because they
have no track record of understanding what it's like in the sector,"
he explains, "You've got to believe primarily in the social mission
to make it happen." On the other hand, he suggests that: "Social
enterprise is full of people who want to take an entrepreneurial
crack at everything, but you've got to temper that with – can you
do something really well?" It quickly becomes clear that for Matt,

the key to the future of the social enterprise sector is in making sure that social enterprises are excellent at what they do – which means being run well.

Leadership in social enterprises involves a number of different skills and mindsets. "You are the sum of your experience," Matt suggests, "and sometimes that can block change." We're talking about the current moves in the public sector to try to change how services are delivered – how will it all pan out, I ask? It may be a time of change for public bodies, but Matt points out that "it's still the same people leading them. Cuts don't bring about change on their own, it's not about the money, it's about the attitudes. It's going to take a generation." In Matt's vision of the future of public services, 20 years seems like the low-end estimate for any substantial change.

So how do you change attitudes? While the NHS might "highlight the difficulty of changing the status quo", Matt is able to give me an example from his own experience of tapping into the experience and skills of the staff at Street League: "I asked, 'What would it look like if we had to take a 25 per cent cut in funds?' Everyone took a sharp intake of breath, but it turned out to be a really good exercise…They all went away and everyone came back to me with the same operating model. So I said 'why are we not doing it already?' A more efficient way of delivering the same outcomes was staring us in the face." As that example highlights, for Matt, the future is about social enterprises having a firm grip on how scalable they are – in both directions. "Say 'scaling' – everybody automatically thinks up…But it has to mean down as well." Matt explains how each part of Street League is built on delivery teams and all of those teams are at different phases of development – with some growing and some shrinking depending on the environment and the funding available. "If the money's not there, the money's not there…" Matt cautions, but he suggests that for social enterprises in the future, particularly if they are operating in volatile economic times, this type of scalability will be vital to their continued presence, providing their social mission in a suitable way for the circumstances with which they are faced.

Matt also suggests that lean social enterprises will be the ones that succeed and spread because they are the ones that are very clear about which activities relate directly to their unique mission. "In the old charity model you'd do loads of things for loads of people. At Street League, we want to be the best at the specific things we do in very specific places… For instance we say 'If you like football and you're out of work, we can help you'…So, for us that's about working through football, rather than sport in general. We need to be focused on what we can do best."

In Matt's vision of the future, there will be a specialist, quality option for every situation, rather than a generic blanket programme mandated by government. "In the future what I'd like to see is a lot of specialist interventions available everywhere. So at Street League we might go for targeted specialist funding to roll out a programme in 14 towns around cities in which we already work, but we'll know that there is also, for instance, an arts programme accessing that funding too."Crucially, in the future, it will be important not only that the option exists, but that people know about it and make use of it: "Technology is changing things" on that front, Matt says, highlighting how much of the way we communicate with social media has already changed in just three or four years. So, 20 years on, if the world goes the way Matt hopes it will, good communication will help everyone know that social enterprises provide excellent, specific, focused and personalised services and they'll know how to use them if they need to.

About Matt Stevenson-Dodd

Matt is a social entrepreneur with a background in youth work and tackling social disadvantage. A former Government Social Enterprise Ambassador, Matt is chief executive of Street League, the charity which changes young people's lives through football. Under Matt's leadership Street League has developed into a dynamic and innovative social enterprise helping the most disadvantaged 16- to 25-year-olds progress into work, education and training.

Prior to Street League, Matt was chief executive of Young Enterprise North West and founder/CEO of Unique Social Enterprise, a multi-award winning social enterprise in Newark, Nottinghamshire. Matt started Unique in 2000 with a group of local young people and a grant from the National Lottery, but went on to develop a range of innovative social enterprises to support the impact of the charity.

Matt is a full-time qualified youth worker, a fellow of the RSA and has an MBA with Distinction from Nottingham University.

About Street League

Street League is a charity which changes young people's lives through football. Originally founded in 2001, they run a unique football and education programme which helps some of the UK's most disadvantaged young people get a job or return to education. Street League deliberately targets the most disadvantaged unemployed young people who are often gang-involved, ex-offenders, excluded from school, have issues with substance misuse or have no future aspirations.

They use the universal appeal of football to develop a dialogue with these hard-to-reach 16- to 25-year-olds, who have been classified as 'NEET' (not in employment, education or training). Their lack of education and opportunity has left many feeling alienated and frustrated.

The first stage involves Street Football – a two-hour football coaching course every week, during which their UEFA-qualified coaches develop relationships with participants and teach communication skills, health and fitness, teamwork, leadership and motivation as well as encouraging them to take the next step in improving their prospects by joining the Academy.

This classroom-based course lasts for a further eight weeks and comprises a series of practical workshops which provide a range of life and employability skills, such as CV writing and mock interviews, supplemented by intensive one-to-one support to enable participants to progress on their chosen path, whether that be further education, training or work.

Three out of four graduates get a job or go back into education, while research has also shown that the Academy produces a significant reduction in re-offending and substance abuse, as well as major improvements in health and general well-being.

However, as the problem of youth unemployment grows, Street League must also expand so that it can continue to rise to the challenge. They operate in London, Glasgow and Newcastle, launched in Manchester (November 2011) and Edinburgh (April 2012), and have plans to expand into more cities.

JENNY SIMS
The power of democracy

'Our participants could sack me if they didn't like what I was doing – it's right that they should have the ultimate say.'

Jenny Sims is the chief executive of Pembrokeshire FRAME Ltd and really believes in the power of democracy and being accountable to the people who matter most – those who use the service. Pembrokeshire FRAME was set up 20 years ago by Jenny, who then worked in the local authority's mental healthcare team. The aim was to set up a project to provide work practice and training to people with and recovering from mental ill health, challenging the idea that people with mental ill health can't work. "This is nonsense," says Jenny, "but people do need a great deal of ongoing support. One person has worked for us for seven years but before that hadn't worked for 30 years – that person still has a mental illness but is supported in managing it."

Early in our conversation, Jenny tells a story that has great significance in the history of Pembrokeshire FRAME. It was originally set up as a charity with a membership consisting of the volunteers and participants and with a board of trustees. The members elect people to represent them on a members' council. The members' council has responsibility in the constitution for the election and dismissal of directors/trustees. In 2000, it was decided that the charity also needed to set up a company limited by guarantee to enable it to recruit directors with more business skills. Jenny was asked to look for new directors and recruited two businessmen and a solicitor. The assets of the business were transferred to the new company but the new board wouldn't accept the transfer of the membership of the charity. "I tried for 18 months to get them to agree but they wouldn't, they didn't think it was important," recalls Jenny. "In the end I went to the members' council. They called an extraordinary general meeting, dismissed the new board members and put in place a temporary chairperson."

After this cathartic moment, Pembrokeshire FRAME grew as a business but has also developed its democratic structures so that participants and volunteers, as represented by the members' council, are firmly in the driving seat. Jenny can't see how social enterprises could work in any other way. "If you're going to remain true to your objectives, how can you not have participants, volunteers and workers involved?" she asks. "It's not without its difficulties," she admits, "but you have to take into account what people want or how do you know you're doing the right things?"

When Jenny talks about her vision for the future of Pembrokeshire FRAME, it is underpinned by the importance of keeping sight of the social mission. "It's not about building an empire, I think we will stay in Pembrokeshire." She returns to the role of the participants and volunteers in the governance of the organisation. "Participants and volunteers don't have a day to day management role, that would be inappropriate and cause chaos. They choose and appoint the directors and are involved in the recruitment of staff. About twice a year the members' council writes to the board and invites them to their meeting. It makes directors stop and think, 'Why am I here?' No director would ever say 'No, I'm not coming.'"

Jenny clearly believes that this involvement of users and other **stakeholders** is what makes them a social enterprise and that when developing more social enterprises in the future, people will need to take this into account. "People on the members' council feel valued and listened to. We also undertake social accounting and regularly seek feedback from people." She thinks that this kind of evidence of the social value of their work is what sets them apart as a social enterprise, as they still struggle to let people know what they do and how they operate.

"When we first set up, we didn't know what we were. My manager in Social Services said early on that we shouldn't depend on getting grants and that grants wouldn't be around for ever – he was a good man and very far-sighted. It was only when someone from Social Firms UK came and said 'You're a social enterprise', that we had a name for what we were. It's still an issue; people don't understand that as a charity we can make profits to re-invest, all our money goes to the people who come here."

Pembrokeshire FRAME operates as a **social firm**. Of their 44 staff, 60 per cent have had some sort of disadvantage, such as mental ill health, a disability or been very long-term unemployed. Jenny says, "We always recruit internally first and we look at people's strengths and abilities, not their disabilities."

Jenny worries that social enterprises will lose their social value if they grow too fast, and lose sight of their social objectives. Her vision for Pembrokeshire FRAME is to offer wider, more varied opportunities to participants during their journey towards employment but also to offer those not able to embark on paid employment worthwhile meaningful occupation – a reason to get up in the morning. Her next move is to try and develop starter units so that participants can develop their own sustainable social enterprises. She has previously been asked to franchise the Pembrokeshire FRAME model but was worried about getting too big and having people take on the franchise who "would do their own thing and not maintain our high standards".

Crucial to the growth of social enterprise is better understanding of what they do. Jenny says that, "You should have to demonstrate very clearly that you are a social enterprise, it's why we do social accounting. It should be possible to tell who is a social enterprise and who isn't. The words 'social enterprise' should be restricted to organisations who are genuinely providing a holistic social benefit to the community." She thinks that what is needed is a proper regulatory framework. "If you're really doing what you say you're doing, then monitoring isn't a problem."

Jenny thinks that in future, social enterprises can and should take on more public sector contracts and that they can offer services that are better value, more person centred and less costly than the public sector, because they are based in and accountable to the community. Over time, she thinks, "people will realise that social enterprises provide high value to their communities, keeping local money local – then we're all winners: the workers, the customers and the community…We have a furniture showroom that is staffed by our participants. People love coming here and our participants love serving them. Everyone FRAME touches is a winner."

About Jenny Sims

Jenny is the managing director of Pembrokeshire FRAME Ltd, her background is in education, small business and mental healthcare. After the birth of her third child Jenny returned to work as an occupational therapist aid on a rehabilitation ward in a large mental hospital in the south of England. It was here that she worked with long-stay patients who were leaving the ward to live in supported accommodation in the community. She met many interesting people with diverse skills and recognised their potential to live fulfilled and rewarding lives given the appropriate support and opportunities. Her experiences led her to challenge the assumption that people who had undergone the trauma of psychiatric illness would be unable to maintain paid employment. Jenny was employed by a Social Services Community Mental Health Team to set up and run a small daycentre for people with and recovering from mental ill health, where she was given the opportunity to try and find a way of overcoming the stigma which often prevented people from entering or returning to paid employment after a period of mental ill health. Over the past 20 years Jenny has gained extensive knowledge and experience through the successful development and management of FRAME as a sustainable and award winning social enterprise.

About Pembrokeshire FRAME

Pembrokeshire FRAME was set up 20 years ago as a route to help people with mental ill health to return to paid employment. With a focus on recycling activities, its aim is to increase the self-confidence and self-esteem of those with a wide range of disabilities who choose to become involved. It has become the vehicle which has enabled hundreds of people to fill a gap in their CV and gain a reference which demonstrates their ability to undertake and sustain paid employment.

FRAME prides itself on its professional approach to running its business and charity. In recent years the organisation has opened its doors to provide its services to all disability groups and also works with people who are considered to be socially disadvantaged. In 2011, with the support of a Welsh Government grant, FRAME purchased and renovated a building which has now become its permanent home, providing the organisation with a secure and sustainable future.

IAIN TUCKETT
The importance of place

'Our main aim is to make life better for everyone who lives, works or studies in our Waterloo and North Southwark neighbourhood.'

Many social enterprises are set up in response to specific issues in a particular area, but if your social enterprise is on the banks of the River Thames in teeming central London, you might expect that there would be less of a focus on the community – but you'd be wrong. Iain Tuckett, CEO of Coin Street Community Builders (CSCB), was one of a group of local residents who led the campaign in the 1970s to build social housing, community facilities and create open space on a prime South Bank riverside site. Iain makes clear that the neighbourhood and locality are just as important to the group today as they were 40 years ago during the campaign to save this space from commercial development.

The campaigners started off trying to get social housing and green open space in the area. They added employment creation as a goal when the major industries in the area (printing and the London Docks) closed. Iain says, "It's stating the obvious now, but someone told us 'Leisure is going to be big.' So we included restaurants and cafés as well as managed craft and design workshops in our development proposals. We argued for mixed and balanced land uses; we sought to create a range of job opportunities; and we included affordable family housing so that the people who service the London economy had somewhere to live. It's all about balance."

Today, CSCB is still building a range of facilities but it also provides integrated programmes of community activities including sports, clubs, and a family and children's centre. Coin Street's opening up of the South Bank riverside has given the public access to what is now one of the most popular walks in London.

One big change, according to Iain, is how they measure what they do. "In the early days it was easy to see the changes we made. We didn't have to measure them; you could see what we were demolishing and what we had built. Now a lot of the work we do is invisible – except to the staff and members of the community involved. So we have had to work out ways to measure it." Nevertheless he points out that "the most important things are the most difficult to measure: things like resilience, self-confidence and creativity".

Reflecting on the lessons learned over the years, Iain emphasises the importance of having a clear vision and sticking to it. Linked to this is building a business model that allows independence from changing government priorities and funding – and from the narrow vision of the market place.

One of the challenges he sees for those building similar social enterprises in the future is the willingness of the public sector to allow embryonic community trusts the opportunity to establish a track record. "Despite all the talk of asset transfers, public bodies are under pressure to sell land to finance their operations and there are few programmes to support new groups in developing robust business plans. This is in contrast with the 1970s when there were active national and local programmes which invested in new housing associations and community ventures. Many of Coin Street's original board members developed their experience by founding housing co-operatives and running community centres. However there are still opportunities, particularly in areas where the private market is inactive or politicians are closely engaged with local groups."

Looking to the future Iain says, "We are currently developing a plan for our next 20 years but the focus is still going to be on our neighbourhood and working in partnership with local organisations and businesses." Being on the South Bank means that local employers include organisations like Shell, St Thomas's Hospital, London South Bank University and the National Theatre. Coin Street played a key role in the early 1990s working with these organisations to form South Bank Employers' Group.

The Rambert Dance Company has just completed its new headquarters and dance studios on Coin Street land and in return offers an extensive community dance programme. Adjacent to Rambert, Coin Street is planning to build a large indoor swimming and leisure centre which will be transferred to Coin Street's charitable arm together with a £20 million endowment to ensure it is sustainable. That development will be funded by building over 200 flats for sale. Elsewhere Coin Street is planning extra care flats and specialist dementia facilities.

Although Iain is happy for CSCB to be described as a social enterprise or as a development trust, he is wary of making too many distinctions based on the legal status of an organisation. "Social enterprise is a brand like creative or cultural industries. It's useful to have but is only of limited value in assessing an organisation. I find discussion of 'public', 'private', and 'third' sectors all very twentieth-century. A small private business has very little in common with a big corporation and neither behaves like a sovereign fund, so why class them together? Likewise many so-called 'public services' are not provided by the public sector."

Having said this, Iain does find it easier to work with other social enterprises, "You can align your objectives better." He also thinks that in the future, social enterprises will be the employers of choice. "If I were a graduate today, it's where I would want to work – for an organisation with social purpose, without shareholders, one that can innovate. People want to work for organisations that are innovative and creative."

Iain believes that an area is more resilient if it involves a wide range of organisations, but, whatever the business model, he believes that the locality, the neighbourhood, needs to be the driver for delivering "mixed and balanced" services. "You can expand locally. You don't have to expand by having franchises and spreading out of the area. You can expand by creating a diverse portfolio of activities and businesses, bringing people together and dissolving boundaries. That's how we innovate."

About Iain Tuckett MBE

Iain is group director of Coin Street Community Builders (CSCB), a development trust and social enterprise which owns and is responsible for developing and managing 13 acres of London's South Bank. Iain has overseen all Coin Street developments to date including the refurbishment of Oxo Tower Wharf for mixed uses; Coin Street neighbourhood centre; Gabriel's Wharf; the completion of the South Bank riverside walkway and laying out of Bernie Spain Gardens; and housing developments for Mulberry, Palm, Redwood and Iroko Housing Co-operatives. CSCB is currently carrying out a major mixed development including a 43-storey housing development, a public swimming and indoor leisure centre, new headquarters and dance studios for Rambert Dance Company, and a new town square.

Iain is deputy chairman of South Bank Employers' Group, a not-for-profit company bringing together 18 major organisations based in the South Bank including Shell International, the London Eye, ITV, Guys and St Thomas's NHS Hospital Trust, Network Rail, Southbank Centre, British Film Institute, National Theatre, Kings College and London South Bank University.

Iain was appointed an honorary fellow of the Royal Institute of British Architecture in 1999 and awarded an honorary fellowship at London South Bank University in 2003 and an MBE for services to architecture and regeneration in 2012.

About Coin Street Community Builders

Thirty years ago the South Bank area of London was bleak, unattractive, had few shops and restaurants, had a dying residential community and a weak local economy. Local residents mounted an extraordinary campaign leading to the purchase of 13 acres of derelict land, since developed into a thriving neighbourhood.

Coin Street Community Builders is a social enterprise and their aim is to make their neighbourhood a great place to live, work in and visit. They have transformed a largely derelict site into a thriving mixed-use neighbourhood by creating new co-operative homes; shops, galleries, restaurants, cafes and bars; a park and riverside walkway; sports facilities; by organising festivals and events; and by providing childcare, family support, learning, and enterprise support programmes. Income is generated from a variety of sources including the hire of retail and catering spaces, event spaces, meeting room spaces and conference venue spaces as well as the provision of consultancy services.

Millions of people enjoy the South Bank Riverside Walkway, the green spaces of Bernie Spain Gardens, and the design shops, galleries, restaurants, cafes and bars at Oxo Tower Wharf and Gabriel's Wharf. An extensive community leisure programme is also run from Coin Street neighbourhood centre and Columbo Centre.

SHAUN DORAN
Beyond an interesting cottage industry to a new wave of social enterprises

'We need to identify and work on the conditions that inhibit the growth of social enterprises.'

"I think social enterprises can make a huge difference on an individual basis. On the other hand, if you look at it against any objective measure, we're only a wrinkle on the face of the way the world works. That's why we need not only small-scale social enterprises doing great stuff, but we also need a new wave of social enterprises to bring that difference to scale," says Shaun Doran, CEO of FRC group. When he compares the organisation he runs to other social enterprises he suggests that with an annual turnover of £5 million, a surplus of around £300,000 and 100 employees it would be considered one of the larger, more established and successful ones in the sector.

Yet, since Shaun has started thinking hard about scale and the extent of the impact social enterprises can make, another comparison has been challenging him to think bigger. "Google almost shares a birthday with us and I think I saw today that they employ 44,000 people, their revenue is measured in billions, their profit in millions. That out-scales anything social enterprise is achieving," says Shaun. "We need to identify and work on the conditions that inhibit the growth of social enterprises."

Throughout our conversation, Shaun is keen to stress that he still thinks that small, locally embedded organisations are capable of doing an important and relevant job. "I admire those social enterprises that say, 'No, this is what we're about, local people, local places'," he says, "but existing organisations need to decide what they're about. If you're about local provision, be about that. If you're about scale, pursue that. Just don't end up being neither one nor the other."

Underpinning Shaun's concept of scaling up is the need for a long hard look at the purpose, resources and trading activities of social enterprises seeking to grow, "You don't want to waste time and money on things that are inherently un-scalable; in the past we've had the input of some people outside the sector advising social enterprises to scale up without understanding what is inhibiting that."

The Furniture Resource Centre grew out of a set of conditions at a particular time, in a specific geographical place and the ideas of particular people. Shaun describes these conditions as "accidentally colliding into a small local charity". While that charity went on to become a successful social enterprise, the organisation has always worked with the partners and resources available at the time to provide furniture cheaply to people who need it. It's a model that continues to work within that context. But partnerships such as those with local authorities are always going to necessitate negotiation and a wider understanding of how political agendas can influence what it is possible to provide.

FRC group's separate new venture works to a different model: "We are going to operate as a weekly payment store, with a light touch credit check, operating on the same terms as the other big payment stores out there [which means allowing people to pay for furniture and other items in instalments], but the only difference is we are in it to get furniture to people cheaply." Shaun describes how this idea developed from trying to avoid inhibitors to growth from the start of the new venture. The idea is that the organisation will be in unmediated contact with its customers, rather than relying on intermediaries or funders: "We're going to have a very direct, honest relationship with our customers. If they like us, we'll thrive. If they don't, we won't."

Going forward, Shaun is optimistic about this new venture because it's built on learning from previous attempts. He hopes the same will be true for others in the social enterprise sector and that a new wave of social enterprises will learn from the successes and failures of previous ones. He advises, "you need to have some real thoughts about your **Mem and Arts** and what they allow you to do. You can always change them, but it indicates a lack of clarity if you suddenly have to change them early on."

He's an advocate of intensive learning for start-ups to give new organisations a chance: "If there are new start-up social enterprises, we need to smother them with as much learning as we can give them." Yet however tolerant he is of start-ups that need to find their way, he is quite blunt about the danger of allowing poor quality social enterprises to continue in the future: "Some social enterprises are rubbish and we don't want the movement to by typified by them and their failures. That's a reality we need to be aware of." He distinguishes between those that are poor quality in their delivery and those that have simply been unfortunate enough to get caught up in a quick change of circumstances. "If a local authority was saying, 'We can't allow X to go out of business because it would look bad,' then that's the wrong decision," Shaun argues, "but if there was a social enterprise that required the funding to help it continue developing more good things, that's a good decision."

Ultimately, in the future, Shaun wants to see both his organisation and the wider sector "talk for itself" in terms of quality and scale of provision. He wants social enterprises to tap into markets where there is a real need and where a workable, scalable social enterprise business model could provide goods and services that people want and charge them appropriately for it. This means learning from big businesses and if necessary, recruiting their staff, just as much as it means being honest about and clearly planning for what your organisation hopes to achieve. So, for Shaun, "The next wave could be the Tescos and Googles of social enterprise." His advice is to remember that scaling up "is not the same as a local grocer deciding to open 1,000 stores. It's different, and we need to use the tools and the learning that helped those bigger businesses get to that scale."

About Shaun Doran

Shaun is CEO of the award winning social enterprise FRC Group where he has been employed since 1999.

Shaun's remit is to ensure that FRC Group's trading companies – Bulky Bob's, Furniture Resource Centre and Revive – create a return against the **triple bottom line** of commercial success, environmental benefit and social dividend.

Additionally, it is Shaun's responsibility to manage the business development programme. FRC Group's ambitious growth programme includes the incremental growth of existing businesses, the creation of new social businesses and the acquisition of, or merger with,private companies and other social enterprises.

Prior to joining FRC Group, Shaun's career was in the timber industry. During this time Shaun managed a number of timber import, export, manufacturing and distribution companies in the UK, Eastern Europe and North America.

Shaun is a graduate of both Liverpool University (Sociology) and Liverpool John Moore's University (Business and Finance) and has studied at Harvard Business School.

About FRC Group

The FRC group encompasses a number of separate but related social enterprise activities which aim both to get great quality furniture to low-income households and to create training opportunities for long-term unemployed people to develop the skills, experience and qualifications they need to gain employment. The group aims to be great for the planet, a great place to work and great to do business with (and works to provide proof that these aims are being fulfilled). The overall mission is to "create profits and opportunities to change the lives of people living in poverty and unemployment".

Within the FRC group these aims are accomplished in different ways, through different social enterprise activities.

The Furniture Resource Centre sells all the items needed to make a house into a home – furniture, appliances, carpets, curtains, even cutlery, bedding and pots and pans. Customers throughout the UK buy a package of products and services from the centre's one-stop shop service to furnish properties from one-bed flats to large shared living developments. Bulky

Bob's is a waste management business running local authority contracts to collect, reuse and recycle bulky household waste – mostly furniture and appliances. Bulky Bob's sells quality 'pre-loved' furniture to low-income shoppers and gives essential items to people in crisis situations free of charge. In Liverpool this happens through Bulky Bob's Furniture World, the city centre store. In Oldham, Bulky Bob's sells furniture from its town centre warehouse and runs 'on the road' events to take these items out to the communities that need them.FRC group shows a strong commitment to understanding, proving and improving the impact – social and environmental – that they make. Every year since 1999 they have produced a report on this topic (developing their process for doing so over time). Unusually within the sector, the report is independently assured by a third party. As a result of this commitment to proving and improving, the group was awarded ACCA/Accountability Award for Best Social Report in 2002 and 2004 and was also shortlisted in the Best Sustainability Report in 2007. In 2009, *Social Enterprise Magazine* called them "the UK's leading social reporters" and listed them as leading the field in measuring social value in three sectors – charities, recycling and training.

Principles and attitudes

In attempting to do business differently, people running social enterprises often stress the values and principles that underpin their approach. However, as these good intentions are often the best understood part of social enterprise, our interviewees are also keen to highlight the need for the right attitude towards business and entrepreneurship.

First, Ed Mayo explains the international co-operative vision for the future, involving accountability, mutual self-help and businesses embedded in their communities.

June O'Sullivan suggests that trading for a social purpose should involve 'high ambition' and attract consumers to the sector by offering tangibly better quality than mainstream competitors.

Working with 'whole' people (rather than just a set of needs) can be combined with dynamic business practices in social enterprises, says Jean Jarvis, and nobody has to be a martyr.

For Tim West, the spirit and culture of the organisation is what makes it a social enterprise, and he suggests that this spirit is precisely why talented young people and mid-life career changers want to sign up to give back to society and provide greater meaning in their lives.

Finally, Brendan Moore suggests that trustworthiness and integrity are key factors influencing the success of small artisan producers, and that acting through a co-op consortium has helped him and other producers demonstrate these qualities to their customers.

ED MAYO

Co-operatives are businesses that are embedded in society

'Accountability isn't a hair shirt, it's a way of getting things done.'

Accountability, self-help, community – these are all words that Ed Mayo returns to throughout our conversation. His thinking is influenced by the international co-operative movement, its experience and visions for the future in different countries and within different economic models. Ed is the secretary general of Co-operatives UK, the national trade body that campaigns for co-operation and works to promote, develop and unite co-operative enterprises. He describes how co-operatives operate a different business model and that this affects everything they do, from the point when a group of people get together to start an enterprise. He tells me that the first step is not to look for external support or a grant but with "self-help and mutual aid. You start with what you've got and then you look around for support, both formal and informal from your family, the community and other social enterprises."

Ed's vision for the future is based on the *Blueprint for a co-operative decade*, published in 2013 by the International Co-operative Alliance. It describes five agreed themes (see below) and Ed says that they are relevant at national and local levels. "It reflects the fact that co-ops are the fastest growing models of enterprise and the preferred model among the general public. The co-op sector is the leader and exemplifier in participation and sustainability." He thinks that how we grow the co-op sector and the wider social economy will address the collective challenges in society of inequality and the constraints of environmental resources.

Ed enlarges on this theme by talking about the strength of the co-op model, how self-help is embedded in social enterprises that are member owned and where there is accountability to members. "It enfranchises those involved in the business, whether that is the workforce, users and customers, enterprise-owned co-ops and multi-stakeholder organisations." He doesn't suggest that all social enterprise should adopt this model, but he says, "What's transformative is the sense of agency – you're an actor involved in making change." Referring to a common assumption that running a business according to democratic principles is difficult and ineffective, he adds, "Accountability isn't a hair shirt, it's a way of getting things done."

One example Ed gives is the **credit union** model. People in the community provide financial services to others, and in the process of doing this, they also build their own and the community's financial skills and confidence.

Developing his vision of the role for social enterprises in the future, Ed describes how they have the potential to influence the wider economy and the way society is viewed. "We tend to think of private sector business as public shareholder-owned organisations, only interested in maximising the return on capital. But there are heterodox business models in the private sector, such as building societies or family-owned businesses. Social enterprises start where it isn't possible to focus on financial returns and that's the model I'm interested in. We have experienced the financialisation of the world, where everything is dominated by finance and the return on capital, where businesses are dancing to the tune of distant investors. But lots of organisations don't operate in that sphere, including co-operatives, mutuals, voluntary organisations, the public sector."

For social enterprises this presents a wider opportunity than winning more business from the state or gaining more of a market share in private sector markets. "It's about building social justice and sustainable livelihoods."

One issue that Ed thinks will not matter in future is the wider understanding of the term 'social enterprise' by the general public. He says that in relation to the general intent and approach of social enterprise there is already a good level of understanding, but he asks "Does the term social enterprise have to become part of the everyday vocabulary?" He points out that the Social Enterprise Mark hasn't created the same level of public awareness as the Fair Trade mark because the public is not aware of the option to have a separate business model to deliver social purpose. In contrast, the fair trade movement was helping to codify an existing concern – that of exploitation of producers in developing countries. Providing a mark offered a tangible solution to a problem people recognised. The Social Enterprise Mark, on the other hand, has been set up to create that awareness. "You have to start with where people are, not tell them they have to use a different language. It's a dead end to assume that a technocratic term has to be widely understood in order for the model to be successful." Finally, Ed returns to the international experience of the co-op sector as an exemplar of how to develop social enterprise in future. He thinks the key is in "second degree co-operation", according to principle 6 of the seven **co-operative principles**, whereby co-operatives work together to grow. "Really successful social enterprises instinctively work together, it's about creating a system of inter-trading and spin-offs for innovation. In areas such as Spain and Northern Italy, social enterprises are embedded in the local economy through working together. The weakness of the Anglo–American version is that they think that it's about creating one more business. What's more important is the way they link up and work together."

The five themes of the Blueprint for a co-operative decade

These five themes comprise the overarching agenda for the ICA, its members and the co-operative sector as set out in the *Blueprint for a co-operative decade*, published in 2013 by the International Co-operative Alliance (p6):

1 elevate participation within membership and governance to a new level
2 position co-operatives as builders of sustainability
3 build the co-operative message and secure the co-operative identity
4 ensure supportive legal frameworks for co-operative growth
5 secure reliable co-operative capital while guaranteeing member control.

About Ed Mayo

Ed Mayo is secretary general of Co-operatives UK. He is a long-term co-operator with a track record of innovation and impact in his work to bring together economic life and social justice.

As chief executive of the National Consumer Council, he was instrumental in mergers leading to the creation of Consumer Focus, the statutory consumer champion, in 2008. Ed rose to prominence as director of the New Economics Foundation, chaired the Jubilee 2000 campaign and was part of the team that founded the Fairtrade Mark. *The Independent* described Ed as "the most authoritative voice in the country speaking up for consumers", while the *Guardian* nominated him as one of the top 100 most influential figures in British social policy.

About Co-operatives UK

Co-operatives UK is the national trade body that campaigns for co-operation and works to promote, develop and unite co-operative enterprises. They operate as a trade association for co-operatives and aim to bring together all those with a passion and interest in co-operative action. They work to promote the co-operative alternative across many sectors of the economy from high street consumer-owned co-operatives to pubs and football clubs, healthcare to agriculture, credit unions to community-owned shops.

Together the co-operative economy is worth some £36.7 billion and the number of co-operative memberships is 15.4 million. Co-operatives are the largest membership movement in the country.

JUNE O'SULLIVAN
Social businesses need to be 'best in class'

'You need to have the ability to explain why you are
different and tell your story.'

June O'Sullivan wants to see more social businesses with "high ambition". She often talks about social businesses rather than social enterprises because she is tired of the debate about social enterprise definitions which, she says, often alienate the public and confuse commissioners. She wants people to understand that social businesses do business in a way that does good. The aim is to create businesses that balance sustainability with social good.

When she became CEO of London Early Years Foundation (LEYF) she demonstrated what high ambition can mean for an organisation. After she was appointed in 2005, the organisation moved from a somewhat traditional charitable set-up to a fully self-sustaining social enterprise. The organisation grew from running nine to 24 nurseries in just eight years – and she hopes that is just the start. June wants LEYF to demonstrate that large and successful social enterprises *are* possible: "I want us to be the biggest childcare social enterprise in the UK and beyond with a reputation that says – yes, you can do this!"

June is adamant that people choose to buy from social businesses "because of what they do, not what they are". For this reason she thinks consumers do not necessarily need to understand the social part of the business when they first encounter the organisation. "My view has always been that people buy our service because it's good and they come to all the social stuff afterwards," June explained. "If you're a social business you want to be 'best in class,'" that is, the foremost business in your field.

However, she does hope that in ten years' time, consumers will be asking more challenging questions about the businesses they buy from as well as seeking out quality. She suggests the way forward for future social enterprises will not be, "coming in and saying 'Ok, did you know we're social?'", but instead demonstrating the additional social value they offer, "You need to have the ability to explain why you are different and tell your story."

For June and LEYF, this difference centres on running a values-led business which places the child at the centre: "I want to create a business that provides a quality experience for children from all backgrounds, because they deserve it. I want every parent who leaves one of our nurseries to say to other parents they meet – 'If you can, go to a LEYF nursery, because they're bloody good.'" June wants to see this type of attitude from future social enterprises – to the point that they aim to be leaders in their chosen business sectors. This will involve really knowing their business sector well.

She wants to see good, large, social enterprises in many sectors, as she believes only this type of exposure will help consumers understand that it is possible to run a quality business with a social purpose: "You need the Body Shop approach, really, to get people to see that you can do things differently. If there was one of us [social enterprise] in every sector, that would help. We need to build some strong brands. We must create a range of businesses in various sectors for people to get the idea." This thriving business model may of course start to involve competition between social enterprises. June has no problem with this idea: "We want to see people out there competing with us. We're not going to get the message out there if there is only one LEYF. I want to see LEYFs in Leeds [and beyond]."

In June's vision of the future, big public and private businesses will see this demonstration of leadership from the social enterprise sector and recognise that they have something to learn from social ways of doing business. She is already trying to bring this vision about when working with big businesses through LEYF: "I've said, don't pat us on the head – you'll learn as much from me as I learn from you. In this way you end up with a much more respectful and reciprocal relationship." Ultimately she hopes that social enterprise leaders will be invited as part of the general business world to show them that there are ways of doing business that are more socially beneficial without compromising the financial bottom line. This is why she was so pleased to be the first childcare business and social business to win the Transforming Change category of the Orange National Business Awards 2012, competing on an open field.

Finally, June O'Sullivan's hope is that social enterprises will be seen by local, national and international policy makers and the business community as operating in just as business-like a way as any mainstream business, but able to do socially beneficial things through the business model. She wants people running social enterprises to be "treated with some dignity, as [people] with values who know what they're doing". Of course, this will necessitate a change in attitude by policy makers and business people: "I want to be with everyone else when [the government] are talking about changing business rules. I don't want to be wheeled in as one of the worthies." However, June also suggests that both practitioners and infrastructure organisations promoting social enterprise will need to adjust how they speak to the world. "Sometimes the way network associations talk about all the good we can do backs us into a corner" June explains. "If we want to sign up for [being taken seriously as businesses] then we can't go running around saying 'Can we have more help?' in a needy way. We want help such as access to finance and working capital in the same way as any business. We need reasonable legislation that does not inhibit business growth but balances fair working practices." While leadership, available growth capital and external attitudes are all important factors in the future growth of social enterprise approaches, June suggests one key thing that will mean the success or failure of any business and of social enterprises going forward: "It's all about knowing your own sector well and doing good by doing business."

About June O'Sullivan

June O'Sullivan is chief executive of the London Early Years Foundation (LEYF). June has been instrumental in achieving a major strategic and cultural shift for the award winning London Early Years Foundation, resulting in increased profile and profitability over the past eight years.

As CEO of the UK's leading childcare charity and social enterprise since 2006, June continues to break new ground in the development of LEYF's scalable social business model. She campaigns to influence policy and make society a better place for all children and families.

June is a speaker, author and regular commentator on Early Years, Social Business and Child Poverty, as well as a champion of community-based, multi-generational projects and a great believer in the potential of greater social and cultural capital as a means of delivering long-term social impact. She continues to advise the government in order to better implement their vision for Early Years.

June is also a fellow of the RSA, director of Earlyarts, trustee for the National Day Nursery Association and chair of Paddington Farm Trust.

About London Early Years Foundation (LEYF)

LEYF is a charitable social enterprise employing over 300 staff across 24 community, workplace and Children's Centre nurseries in London, many in some of the city's most deprived areas.

They aim to make a real difference to the lives of more than 2,300 children and their parents every year, helping them develop a passion for learning, regardless of their background. They operate across six London boroughs – Barking & Dagenham, Camden, Kensington & Chelsea, Lambeth, Tower Hamlets and Westminster.

They are also committed to helping disadvantaged young adults realise their own potential. Every year they recruit around 20 people to their Early Years apprenticeship scheme, which develops their vocational and interpersonal skills, leads to a Diploma for the Children and Young People's Workforce, and offers the opportunity to start their career in childcare with LEYF.

Finally, an all-embracing community ethos means 'doing good' doesn't stop at the nursery door, as their multi-generational and partnership-led approach helps to enrich the natural strength and qualities of each local community they serve.

JEAN JARVIS
Working with the whole person

'We collect and restore furniture – and in a way
we collect and restore people too.'

Jean Jarvis is the founder and chief executive of The Furniture Scheme, but her main motivation has always been to help people. Initially this took the form of providing furniture for people on a low income. Over the years the social enterprise has developed to provide training and employment for local people and recently started to manage two community centres. Jean explains this expansion as "enabling us to work with the whole person, not just their need for furniture".

The Furniture Scheme started off as a charity, collecting furniture for redistribution but soon found that they were being given more valuable pieces and the best way to help people was to sell these for a profit and spend the money helping people in different ways. "We recruit our staff locally," says Jean. "Although some people start in low-skilled jobs, we like to train and promote them into management if they show potential. Maria came to us as a volunteer from the local community and then became a trainee on the Future Jobs programme. We provided training and development and now she manages two community centres."

Having run the furniture scheme for some years, Jean was beginning to think about having more of a presence in the community when she was approached to take on two failing community centres. The Furniture Scheme is already turning the centres round and Jean's aim is for them to be self-sustaining in five years. Like the furniture recycling, the centres are "creating a place where people can come and find their niche".

With this focus on developing people, Jean has found innovative ways of growing the business to be able to offer more services to more people and she sees working in partnership as being critical to being able to expand. She has successful partnerships with other charities, local authorities, a large housing association and Veolia, an international private enterprise. She believes that it is her success in finding partners and working with them that helps her to continue to fulfil her mission. Jean's vision of how social enterprises will develop and grow in the future is based on this experience of how her own social enterprise has grown. She thinks that in future, social enterprises will have to develop more relationships. She has invested a lot of time in helping her partners to understand the role of the social enterprise and how it can help them to achieve more. The housing association wanted to do more 'social enterprise stuff' but Jean says they didn't know how to go about it. Now the partnership delivers more services to the tenants and she works closely with the chief executive who can see the benefit of working with a specialist provider. Jean points out that, "Anyone leading a social enterprise will want people to understand what it is, and that's important." She also had to raise awareness at Veolia, where The Furniture Scheme is sub-contracted to collect bulky waste and deliver recycling bins in South Shropshire as part of an integrated waste contract for the council. "At first they thought that it would be volunteers that would be doing the work and were worried that they might not turn up on time." There were financial penalties for Veolia if the contract targets weren't met so Jean had to demonstrate that "We run our business like anyone else. We did lots of work to prove we could do it and to build trust. We knew that the contract wouldn't make that much money and we were being watched by others in the sector. But we knew there would be spin-offs and that more would come if we built a relationship."Describing a range of new plans for the future of the business, Jean makes it clear that it is vital to have an entrepreneurial approach. "I was disappointed because I thought I could convert everyone to running a social enterprise. You must be able to spot opportunities, take risks and move fast. But lots of people are frightened of risks and of losing money. People came to visit us to learn from our experience and I said to them 'Could you work with someone like me?' Most of them said 'No'." However, she has found overlapping interests in surprising places: "We have a multimillionaire on one of our boards and he loves developing people in his business, so we're not that far away from each other."

Jean thinks that it is important for the organisation to be recognised as a social enterprise but that this will matter less over time as all business will be run in this way. However, when asked about the risks for social enterprises in the future she sees the main one as financial.

"Social enterprises are always on the brink. We've never managed to build up reserves. If we've got it, we spend it on our social purpose. We're always teetering on the brink of failure. Nothing we do makes huge profits. I was a Social Enterprise Ambassador and we were all struggling with the finances. A few do really well but it's only to reinvest the money in the business. The real risk is the failure of the business and the risk to the reputation of social enterprise. It's like women going into business, you have to prove you can do it. People are quick to grab failures and say that social enterprise doesn't work."Jean thinks that the other risk to the reputation of social enterprises is people jumping on the bandwagon. "There are silly things like leisure centres that think that one small social activity makes them a social enterprise. But there are dodgy people everywhere." A solution is to invest in quality standards, especially the Social Enterprise Mark, which "shows that you're a good social enterprise". Government initiatives to raise awareness, such as the Social Enterprise Ambassadors programme, also help. Jean thinks that these exercises in brand recognition will become increasingly important in the future. Ultimately, she says, "We need to prove ourselves as businesses over time. Our contract with Veolia is for 27 years and we had to prove that we were trustworthy and wouldn't let them down."Jean's energy and vision have clearly helped her to develop her business, people in the community and the important relationships she has with her partners. She is totally committed to social goals, and yet, she says, "I'm a businesswoman – I got an MBE for it and I love all that. I love what I do and I can do so much in the community. I'm in a paid job, I'm not a martyr to the cause." Jean is keen to spread the word that being part of the social enterprise movement isn't about putting on a hair shirt, but adds, "People are supposed to go into business to give themselves a better life. With me, it's to give other people a better life!"

About Jean Jarvis MBE

Jean is co-founder and chief executive of The Furniture Scheme, which started in 1994 as a voluntary organisation and now employs 40 staff and manages two community centres. She is also co-founder of the Revive Group. Jean was one of the 25 Social Enterprise Ambassadors through a government-led programme to raise the national profile of social enterprise. She is a member of the Social Enterprise UK Council and was honoured with an MBE in 2011 for services to social enterprise. Jean is also a director of FRN. The Furniture Scheme joined the Wrekin Housing Group as a partner in April 2013, where Jean leads on social enterprise.

About The Furniture Scheme

The Furniture Scheme is a leading social enterprise with a mission to enhance the quality of life of disadvantaged people, by providing access to low cost furniture and improving employment related skills through training and mentoring. FUSE, the scheme's social enterprise development agency, has supported over 300 social enterprises and charities to date through its expertise in all things entrepreneurial.

TIM WEST

Social enterprises: helping people at work remember that they are human beings

'More people want to have a career that is responsible,
to balance selfishness and selflessness.'

Tim West is usually doing the interviewing. He runs Matter&Co, a media and market building business that specialises in working with a variety of organisations that combine enterprise with a social mission. For 12 years he has edited *Social Enterprise* magazine (now *Pioneers Post*) and now has a wide ranging client group that includes large private sector businesses that want to pursue social goals, public sector bodies as well as social enterprises. For this reason, his definition of social enterprise is wider than many people's: "I think social enterprise is a verb, not a noun. It's about combining an innovative, entrepreneurial spirit and solid business management expertise, in order to drive forward your social mission and purpose. It's not about legal structures though this can be important, particularly in relation to governance issues, but I believe it's the spirit and culture of the organisation that defines it, rather than its legal structure." Although this definition is very broad, Tim qualifies it by saying that three things are important to protect the integrity of social enterprises: transparency, governance and proving the impact of what you do. Naturally we spend a large part of our conversation discussing the implication of this definition, starting with what business support is needed by social enterprises. Tim thinks that business support tends to be defined by governments, which decide what is needed and then businesses have to fit into this model. This has happened with successive governments and at the moment the big ideas are investment readiness and public sector spin outs as mutuals, so this is the support that is available. Tim thinks that what is missing is generic business support as previously provided by Business Links, and higher level support for mature social enterprises, although he thinks this is increasingly offered by universities and business schools. He is clear that while building general business expertise should be the core focus, the business side must be reconciled with the social purpose of the organisation: "People need to develop more confidence to talk about social purpose. We're not there yet but we need to develop ways of creating the narrative about the social side of the business."

Tim's vision of the future role for social enterprise is that it becomes a known part of mainstream business culture. Currently, he thinks, we have what people understand by business, and what people understand by charity. There is a tension between them and a risk of them pulling further apart. Social enterprises can create a natural bridge in response to this tension. Business schools have started to discuss social enterprise in their teaching and Tim thinks that students are attracted by the opportunity to work to pursue social goals as well as money. "More people want to have a career that is responsible, to balance selfishness and selflessness. Mainstream business doesn't give people the feeling that they're doing something worthwhile, whereas social enterprises create this opportunity to make the world a better place."

I asked Tim where this leaves the public sector. Traditionally people who wanted to work for public good rather than private wealth worked in the public sector. Tim agrees but says that the public sector is increasingly seen as a bad thing and needs some social innovation. "We don't necessarily need to spin out services to be more entrepreneurial. We need to encourage dynamic and innovative people in the public sector, they can learn from social enterprises how to develop innovation and investment, using money better – that could be really exciting."

Tim has worked with some public sector mutuals and is concerned that some of them are being set up with unrealistic expectations. "Too many of them waste money keeping going and they are not really meeting their social goals. We need the right level of thinking about how to keep entrepreneurial skills within the public sector. The sectors are different but they need to learn from each other."

Tim thinks that what is needed in all these areas is a wholesale change of culture "People are only judged in their jobs according to how well they meet their budgets. The blunt tool of the market place is not right for everything." People need to understand the different roles and functions of public, private and charitable organisations and the balance between social goals and profit. He goes on to say that, "Your definition of success depends on your primary goal. I don't see the public sector disappearing but I think more and more services will be delivered by social enterprises and charities."

In order for this to happen, Tim thinks that, "We need to give contracts to people who can prove the social value of what they do through social impact measurement. I'd like to see standard principles that are measured across the sectors, social accounting needs to develop a standard approach the same way that normal accounting does. We need standard metrics for social impact."

This shouldn't exclude small organisations. Tim gives the example of a collaboration between 24 community transport organisations in London that were co-ordinated by ECT, a very large provider, to deliver accessible transport throughout the capital for the 2012 Olympics. The contract was offered by Transport for London (TfL) when the market failed and TfL described the delivery by the consortium as "exemplary". Tim says that this sort of recognition will enable social enterprises to gain more media coverage and this will help them to join the mainstream.

Tim thinks that those three issues: transparency, impact and governance will become more visible to people when they make choices about where to work and where to buy. "You need to show that you're authentic by what you do and how you do it. Some people undermine social enterprise by being greedy and doing bad things, so we need to be comfortable about transparency and impact. This is especially true when it comes to social enterprise failure. We need to be more mature and acknowledge and learn from failure – and one failure doesn't mean that social enterprise doesn't work."

Ultimately, Tim keeps returning to the subject of business meeting people's personal goals and values or the mark they make on the world. "Big businesses are full of people who want to make a living but most people also want to do good and are aware of social injustice.

Social enterprises can catalyse this desire and can develop a model of businesses for social change, challenging the traditional sectors and helping to remind people that they are human beings."

About Tim West

Tim West has been working in the space where business and social mission meet for well over a decade. He leads mission-focused public relations and marketing agency Matter&Co, is founder of Good Deals, the UK's foremost social investment conference, and is founding editor of *Pioneers Post*, an online newspaper and learning platform connecting social innovators across the globe. With Royal Bank of Scotland he created the RBS SE100 Index of high-growth, high-impact social businesses – a market intelligence tool that aims to help social businesses prove their worth as mission-focused businesses.

Tim is a trained journalist, has a degree in music from the University of Oxford and studied business at Warwick and Cranfield. He is a director of Big Issue Invest, a leading UK impact investor; a trustee of ECT, one of the UK's leading transport charities; an advisor to Deloitte's groundbreaking Social Innovation Pioneers programme; and serves on the UK Council of the SROI Network.

BRENDAN MOORE

Helping small businesses develop through a
co-operative consortium

'The co-op provides trust and integrity.'

Brendan Moore is one of the founders of the East Anglian Brewers'
Co-operative (EABC), a consortium of microbreweries that work
together to improve the quality of their products and to reach new
markets. Brendan runs his own microbrewery, Iceni, based near
Thetford in Norfolk and started to work with other small brewers in
2002 when they realised that there were opportunities to deliver each
other's beer and share resources such as bottling plants, which would
keep their costs down and enable them to be more competitive.

This approach is known as a co-operative consortium, which is set
up by a group of small businesses, and is described by Co-operatives
UK as a way to "save money, spread risk, and enable the participating
businesses to pool their resources, provide mutual support and
learning and strengthen their business sector, while maintaining their
business independence".

Over the years, EABC has developed and so has its mission.
According to Brendan, EABC now aims "to develop a new and
profitable market place for beers – outside pubs". He goes on to
explain how the co-operative is working to take brewing to a new
level, inspired by 'extreme beers' produced in Italy and the United
States. The co-op has created a scheme called 'Extraordinary Ales'
which is changing the business model of brewing.

"We noticed that there was a luxury market for other drinks, for wines and spirits, but not for beer. We'd come across extreme beers in the US and Italy and we knew that they were growing in Holland and Spain, and we thought, 'Why not here?'"

Brendan's vision for the future is based on the co-op's attempt to change the business model for microbreweries. He explains that conventional brewing in the UK aims to "make beer as cheaply as possible, sell as much of it as possible and charge as much as possible". Although small brewers such as Brendan and his fellow co-operators attempted to produce artisan beers in small quantities, they were at the mercy of suppliers who were geared up to produce on a large scale for the big brewers. "It was difficult for us to get our own barley separated so we could demonstrate which farm it came from, maltsters wouldn't separate it for us. We were essentially getting the same product as big breweries but paying more for it." He goes on to explain that in Britain the profit in beer is dependent on the worst beer being sold, "the last beer in the barrel, the bottles at the end of their shelf life – you must sell all that to make your profit".

Things changed in 2010 when the co-op members went to Italy to visit 'extreme' brewers and they had an intern from the US. "We learned that we could produce rare beers in small amounts. We found that 300 was the 'reach number' we should aim for – the typical number of people in a club or the number of friends people have on Facebook is 150, so the 'reach' is the number of people you can contact directly and tell the story of your beer." Brendan illustrates this by telling the story of the first beer that was produced in this way. "Lots of pubs are called The Chequers, but it doesn't have anything to do with the game. The name comes from the chequers tree, which produces a fruit that was traditionally used to preserve beer. They are rare nowadays, but with the help of a local tree enthusiast, we found one and used the berries in the traditional way. This first beer was made in a larger quantity but we found that interest dropped off after we'd sold 300 bottles. We decided that this was the natural limit of people who knew the person who'd found the tree – they were the ones who would care about the story and be prepared to spend £9.50 on the beer."

The co-op members began to take more care over how they sourced their ingredients and looked for small quantities. One brewer picked wild hops that he found using Google Earth, and made a small, unique brew from this local produce. Brendan says that all the areas that are famous for good quality brewing and wine growing have strong local federations, "In Modena, Bordeaux and the Napa Valley in California the producers have a common cause and are working for the right reasons to make the best products. The co-op is our federation. It has enabled us to bid for funding to invest in developing these products and to negotiate better deals with suppliers." A further benefit is that the co-op reinforces the message they need to send out to customers – that this is a different way of doing business and is based on trust. "British brewers aren't trusted because of the tradition of producing cheap beer." To charge the prices they need to make a profit on small quantities, they need to be trusted. "The co-op provides trust and integrity, it gives us a structure to develop this approach and we can access funders who wouldn't give to individual businesses."

As a small, artisan producer, Brendan wants to change the business model for his own brewery and those of his colleagues. "We have to be able to spend more time selling to the customer, because we have to tell the story each time. It is how most small businesses start, in a small way and with passion. Not all businesses can be big but sometimes it feels like the only measure of success is if you're selling to supermarkets. We have to change that and our co-op is proving that other ways work."

For Brendan, working together with others who share this passion has changed his business – and his whole life. "In the early days I was just chained to the machine trying to produce as much beer as possible, I was working 12-hour days and didn't have time to speak to customers or drink the beer. Now I'm living the life people always thought I was."

About Brendan Moore

Brendan is the owner and manager of Iceni brewery, which is situated on the edge of the Thetford Forest, in the Brecklands area of Norfolk. The name Iceni is derived from the Iceni tribe who were ruled by Queen Boudicca and occupied most of Norfolk and Suffolk around AD 61.

Brendan previously worked in the food industry and set up his brewery in 1995. He now brews a range of 36 beers, some of which are seasonal, with names such as Boudicea Chariot Ale, Fen Tiger, Thomas Paine Porter and Deirdre of the Sorrows (the latter reflecting his Irish origins). He now runs a shop attached to the brewery and provides guided tours for visitors. He is one of the founder members of the East Anglian Brewers Co-operative.

About East Anglian Brewers Ltd

East Anglian Brewers Ltd (EAB) is a brewers' co-operative founded in 2002 as a company limited by guarantee. With plenty of sunshine and a lower annual rainfall than Jordan, the farmers of the eastern counties of England grow some of the best malting barley in the world. With such a wonderful raw ingredient on their doorstep it is not surprising that brewers in East Anglia are becoming established as some of the finest brewers in Europe.

EAB offers the discerning drinker a wide choice of brewing styles from smooth dark stouts and porters to refreshing lagers or specialised seasonal beers. By networking with local farmers, EAB aims to produce beers brewed with local malts and to make the ales available to local communities through farmers' markets and community shops. The co-op has 50 members, all of whom are micro-breweries in the region.

Involving the people

One of the fault lines within social enterprise debates has been over whether greater involvement of beneficiaries, employees and communities in social enterprises is a vital part of their distinctiveness or a distraction from growing larger and doing more. The following pieces demonstrate how even those who do want to 'involve people' mean very different things by it – politically, philosophically and in practice.

Jeremy Nicholls suggests that social enterprises that make the effort to take into consideration the views of their different stakeholders are part of a wider movement for business accountability. It's a movement to make sure all organisations think about the consequences of their actions for everyone they might affect.

Employee ownership on a large scale is possible, argues Margaret Elliott, and it brings with it benefits for the employees and the users.

Jesse Norman resists the idea that involving people in the businesses they work for or use is essentially a left wing idea and hopes that in the longer term a wider variety of business leaders and politicians will realise its potential.

Jim Brown describes practical ways to make sure that when involvement is important, people are given more than a 'sense' of ownership and actually have a real say and stake in organisations.

JEREMY NICHOLLS
Accountability now

'Power corrupts... so how do you remove this corrosive effect?'

There are two distinct courses Jeremy Nicholls thinks social enterprise could take in the future. It could remain "a small sector that's very innovative at turning needs into demand" (with more mainstream companies delivering on that demand once it has been identified) or it could become "a way of radically restructuring the economy around a better level of accountability". Given Jeremy's early training as an accountant and consequent wide-ranging professional experience in finding ways to account for social value, it is hardly surprising that most of our subsequent discussion focuses on the latter option. Key to his vision of the future is not only that businesses intend to create social change, but that they are also *willing to prove it*.

"We already have a hugely effective process of determining a business' proof and intent – it's called financial accounting. But it's no longer fit for purpose," Jeremy asserts. As we talk, the reason he gives for this is that financial accounting only provides partial information on the overall effects of the organisation and its activities. The social value, to those who work for the organisation, buy from it, sell to it or live near it is simply not part of the official accounting process. In Jeremy's future vision, taking account of the experience of these people would be an integrated part of the accounting and audit process: "Surely if you are thinking about understanding the material effects of your organisation you will have to involve the stakeholders who experience those material effects of the organisation's work." He's keen to see that "accountability is for anyone your organisation might affect".

"For me, it's always been about reducing inequality," Jeremy explains. "A market economy is not always working in the interests of consumers. Power corrupts…so how do you remove this corrosive effect?" Jeremy's answer, put simply, was that if people who were affected by the organisation were given a greater voice, it could change what constitutes profit and success for that organisation.

Playing devil's advocate, it's possible to suggest that there are other ways of holding organisations to account. What about the law, for instance? "We often assume that law or direct ownership is adequate," Jeremy explains, "But it's very slow. Think of the speed of government systems. You can be 20 years in a class action suit."

According to Jeremy, speeding up the accountability process comes from embedding approaches to stakeholder feedback into accounting requirements: "What you need are accountability processes that force that type of accountability now." Jeremy's vision is one where an auditor would pick up on the ways organisations were choosing what to listen to. "I'm not sure you can expect legislative changes to keep up with the changes that are required. That's why I'm a fan of audit. If an accountability framework includes knowing about who you affect, auditors can come in, take a view, and if they say, 'We're not signing your accounts,' then the shares are de-listed. There are two very fast ways to get a company accountable – customers stopping buying things and de-listing it. It's a fast response."

It's been clear throughout the interview that Jeremy is advocating the change towards evidencing social effects in the whole of the business community, not just in social enterprises. In this wider context there are already developments such as the International Integrated Reporting Council. However, as we turn our attention back towards accountability in social enterprises, Jeremy highlights a potential area for confusion: the difference between the linked ideas of investigating impact to inform management effectiveness and investigating it to ensure accountability.

There are currently pressures on social enterprises and charities to demonstrate that they are delivering the outcomes which they say they are. But it is important to identify how moves in this direction differ from the type of accountability Jeremy is proposing: "We need to understand the difference between judging management effectiveness and accountability," Jeremy suggests. He contrasts an organisation that asks "Are we performing against our mission effectively?" and only therefore checks for success against "aims A, B and C" and the one that asks, "In pursuing those objectives, what else happened?" The distinction Jeremy is making is between an organisation that focuses solely on its own ability to carry out a specific task, which is management effectiveness, and another that finds ways of exploring how its operations (not just those designed specifically to do good) affect the world for good or ill, which is a wider sense of accountability.

This all means that Jeremy thinks many civil society organisations could become more accountable and that boards have some catching up to do in overseeing the social value being created in their organisations: "I suspect that most social enterprise boards don't know if they are maximising social value or could be creating more with their resources." In part this may be due to the differences around scale and visibility, in that many social enterprises are smaller businesses so face less public exposure than larger corporations. It is also important to remember that accountability mechanisms of the open market – for example, consumer choice – don't work where there is little or no real choice available. "In organisations dealing with inequality, where resources are constrained…the people being served cannot so easily go somewhere else for that service. This means the board has a role to ensure that the organisations looks at the service from the perspective of a beneficiary."

Although there is of course much more to do in the sector to bring about his vision of the future, Jeremy reminds me that there are already a growing number of social enterprises that recognise the importance and value of a wider accountability and they are beginning to share their experiences, for example, through RBS 100 (see page 97).

About Jeremy Nicholls

Jeremy Nicholls is the chief executive of the Social Return on Investment (SROI) Network, which is a membership organisation for individuals, organisations and companies supporting principles and standards in accounting for social and environmental value. In this role he advises public, private and voluntary sector organisations on how they can increase the value created by their work.

He is a director of ShareAction, a director of the FRC Group (a social business based in Liverpool), the chair of the Social Impact Analysts Association, a director of Social Evaluator (an online platform for the analysis of social returns) and a member of the IRIS advisory committee. He lectures at several universities including the Said Business School at Oxford University and Hult International Business School.

He has written *There is no business like social business* with Liam Black, *More for your money: A guide to procuring from social enterprises* with Justin Sachs and worked with others to write a number of SROI guides including, most recently, the UK government-supported *Guide to SROI*.

About the SROI Network

The SROI Network promotes the use and development of the Social Return on Investment methodology internationally, encouraging a community of practice along the way. The SROI Network is a membership organisation and a company limited by guarantee. The objectives of the SROI Network are:

- to ensure the principles and standards of SROI are adhered to;
- to develop the methodology;
- to disseminate information on indicators and proxies for use in SROI analyses;
- to train SROI practitioners and provide peer support.

SROI is an approach to understanding and managing the value of the social, economic and environmental outcomes created by an activity or an organisation. It is based on a set of principles that are applied within a framework. The seven principles are:

1 Involve stakeholders
2 Understand what changes
3 Value the things that matter

4 Only include what is material
5 Do not over-claim
6 Be transparent
7 Verify the result

SROI seeks to include the values of people that are often excluded from markets in the same terms as used in markets, that is money, in order to give people a voice in resource allocation decisions. SROI is a framework to structure thinking and understanding. It's a story not a number. The story should show how you understand the value created, manage it and can prove it.

MARGARET ELLIOTT
Creating sustainable jobs and high quality care

'People working in businesses should own them.'

A company in a sector notorious for low pay and a high staff turnover has created loyalty from its staff and customers, because the employees own and control the business.

Sunderland Home Care Associates was set up 20 years ago in a former mining community by Margaret Elliott and Shaun Jackson. Today Margaret is director of Care Services and the business employs 460 staff who really do own the business.

When I ask her what the mission of SHCA is, Margaret says that they have had the same mission statement for years and it is very simple, "to provide the best jobs possible for the workers and to provide the best quality services for users". Margaret believes that these two factors go hand in hand and because the workforce is valued and listened to, they have been able to deliver high quality services. This view underpins her vision of how support for poor and vulnerable people can be delivered in future.

SHCA was originally set up as a worker co-operative, but in 2000 they converted the co-operative into an employee-owned social enterprise. They wanted to be able to give financial rewards to the workers, so they set up an employee benefit trust and created a share incentive scheme.

"Once we know how much profit we've made, we invest in the terms and conditions of staff, including training, and also in the employee benefit trust. It's only the workers who can own shares, which are free. There are no outside shareholders." Margaret describes how this helps staff in what is still a relatively low paid industry to be able to cash in their shares if they need to. "We didn't want to lose staff if the only way you could sell your shares was if you left the company. So one day a year we have a regulated shares market." The first year that this took place the shares were valued at £2.50 each (by the HMRC and SHCA's auditor). Now they are worth £9.50 each. "It's a nice little nest egg, and a good way for staff to own a piece of the company."

The staff also elect the board of directors. Margaret believes that this democratic structure means that they give of their best all the time. "If they see someone doing something they don't like, they say something, because they think, 'It's our company.'" At a time when some care services are under scrutiny because of concerns about quality, this model could be extremely influential in future.

Margaret thinks that diversification is critical to secure the future of social enterprises, particularly in sectors like care when they are delivering public services under contracts. "If we don't win the tender then the workers could be out on their ear…unless it was a TUPE[1] situation, but they wouldn't want to TUPE to a non-social enterprise company." However, diversification enables SHCA to redeploy staff if they fail to win a tender. From the core service of providing home care, SHCA now runs a garden centre, a café, provides academic support to Sunderland University and learning mentors to Sunderland Colleges and runs a holistic support service for people with learning disabilities who gain work experience in some of the other ventures. Margaret says that psychologists who work with the latter group have commented that the participants have changed. "We said, well of course they've changed. If you give people somewhere to live, something to do, provide support systems and enable them to earn a little bit of money, people will change."

When I asked Margaret whether she thinks that the boundaries will be blurred between the public, private and social enterprise sectors in future, she says they already are. As publicly funded services are cut back, social enterprises are the obvious way forward. "Public services are not the best at being flexible and thinking on their feet. Social enterprises are quicker at making decisions and once people get a flavour of working this way, they become more innovative and less constrained. People have got a lot to give if they're not constrained by bureaucracy." This is increasingly being recognised, "People are starting to take notice that continuity of employment leads to improved quality of care."

The threats to this model are already being faced by SHCA. Their competition in the market place is from "massive private enterprises". Margaret acknowledges that there has to be competition, but sees the risk of prices being forced down, evidenced by the fact that their staff have not had a pay rise for five years. She also says that there is danger from the old fashioned co-op image of sandals and lentils. "We need to be more hard-nosed and business-like, which will create a more professional image."

Margaret has taken very practical steps to address this issue and to spread the word about their way of working. She is one of the founders of Care and Share Associates (CASA), which was set up to replicate the SHCA model in other areas. The aim is not only to make quality services available elsewhere but to enable SHCA to "scale up and give the big guys a run for their money". She believes that replication of successful businesses like SHCA will strengthen the social enterprise sector. The CASA model has also had the benefit of not putting SHCA at risk. She confesses that "it's been lots of hard work but it's sailing now".

Margaret has taken the SHCA message all over the world. She has spoken at a conference in Australia and says "We're very big in Japan, we're in books and they think highly of our ideals."

Over 20 years, SHCA's ambitions have grown based on the belief in and success of their model that puts the staff at the heart of the business. "People working in businesses should own them. There are lots of models of social enterprise and there is not a right or wrong way of operating, but we love this model and we really think it works. It's daft not asking the people who are doing the work, how it could be improved."

Note

[1] Transfer of Undertakings Protection of Employment law where new contract holders are obliged to take on the staff of the previous contract holder.

About Margaret Elliott OBE

Margaret Elliott has been involved in co-operative/employee-owned development since the 1970s, first as founder member of a worker's co-operative shop, Little Women, and then in a small Home Care co-operative, Little Women Household Services Ltd. This co-op used social security benefits to cover the cost of the help. It built up close contacts with social services, trade unions and the voluntary sector.

After a stint at the Prince's Trust and a study visit to care co-operatives in New York, Margaret established the hugely successful Sunderland Home Care Associates in 1994. It received the UK Social Enterprise of the Year award in 2006. Currently, SHCA employs over 420 people and has an annual turnover of £5.3 million. Margaret is also a founder member of Care and Share Associates (CASA). CASA develops companies based on the SHCA model. There are currently six companies that have been developed and are supported by CASA's Social Franchise model. For more on CASA see Guy Turnbull's interview below.

Margaret's commitment to participation in the workplace is as strong now as it was when she first learned of this totally different way of working in the early 1970s. Margaret's dedication and achievements were recognised with the award of an OBE in 2009. She is regularly invited to participate in discussions on the shaping of government policy in areas of social enterprise, mutualisation and employee ownership. Margaret's way of working will continue to inform the development of Sunderland Home Care Associates and CASA.

About Sunderland Home Care Associates (SHCA)

On 4 July 1994 SHCA started providing a personal care service to the vulnerable people of Sunderland in their own homes. The service was to help people remain independent in their own homes for as long as possible. It evolved from two previous co-operatives set up by Margaret Elliot and Robert Oakeshott – both aiming to create employment opportunities for women in Sunderland. SHCA was able to take advantage of changes to the way local government arranged home care in the 1990s and they have won a number of contracts, initially from Sunderland City Council and later from other authorities in the North East.

SHCA was initially set up as a worker co-op to enable all the workers to share ownership and control of the organisation for which they worked. In 2000 it converted into an employee-owned company so that the staff could benefit from the value of shares in the business with an 'Internal Regulated Share Market'.

In 2009 they developed Independent Futures: a partnership venture with Health and Adult Services. SHCA is supporting people with learning disabilities who have been in long-stay units and assisting them to find and live in their own homes. So far they have 26 people living in their own homes supported by well qualified and committed staff.

They also work in partnership with the Registered Social Landlord, Gentoo, in the Cherry Tree Gardens complex, providing 24-hour care to the residents of the building. This extra care complex is a state of the art, beautiful building. The complex includes seven bungalows in which they also provide care.

They work with Sunderland Council to develop 'Cafe on the Park' in Herrington Country Park, and employ people with learning disabilities. They believe that this may be the first time a person with a learning disability will have shares in their own company.

Starting off with 20 carers, recruited to deliver their first contract, SHCA now employs over 450 people. In 2004 they set up a company, Care and Share Associates Ltd (CASA) so that they could replicate their model in other areas. Their aim is to democratise home care services across the north.

JESSE NORMAN MP
A future shaped by the models that succeed

'The idea that co-ops are intrinsically left wing is nonsense.'

Jesse Norman MP has argued for 'compassionate economics' and 'real capitalism' in a series of short books and pamphlets that focus on the role of culture and values in market economies. He would also like to see a larger and more socially prominent social enterprise sector involved in a wide variety of business areas, and he is open to the many forms those social enterprises could take: "Disputes over nomenclature are taken to be important to policy formation, which they rarely are...My view is simple: [a social enterprise is] an organisation whose purpose is social good." Within this view he incorporates not only civil society organisations such as charities and community associations, but also co-ops, mutuals, employee-owned businesses, trusts and more.

A Conservative member of parliament, Jesse is adamant that "The idea that [for instance] co-ops are intrinsically left wing is nonsense." He suggests that social enterprises exhibit characteristics such as thrift, private energy, autonomy from the state, connections with self-help in communities and a "small platoon quality", all of which he disputes are necessarily associated with socialism. He particularly highlights a feeling of immense energy within the current social enterprise sector, despite its current size.

As long as the UK social enterprise sector remains small, Jesse suggests, the difference this approach can make to the lives of UK citizens remains "fairly modest". However, he believes that the energy in the sector at the moment may lead to emerging models paving the way for a larger and more established market share. "The appetite is large because we're going through a crisis of capitalism," Jesse offers, but admits that the integration of large numbers of social enterprises into the economy will probably be a long-term project. When asked if social enterprises would join the mainstream, Jesse is clear on both the possibility and the wait required: "Not for a long time, but does that mean it's not worth doing? – No, of course it doesn't."

In the meanwhile, Jesse focuses on two key things that could help support the developing sector. First, he warns that there is not enough expert advice available: "There is a lack of a large cadre of professional advisers for those hoping to set up social enterprises or to develop them." This advice is needed because of the unconventional nature of organisations that are tailored to the purpose of providing social good through business means. Jesse notes: "It is widely recognised that because they are unusual institutions, they are different, they exhibit a complexity of legal form" and this complexity means that it is harder for people both inside and outside of them to understand what they do. According to him, the key thing for a government to do is to foster an environment where professional support is recognised as a business opportunity that the market can provide and in which new start-ups or developing organisations will recognise the need to invest. Jesse suggests certain ways of changing the business environment which will lead businesses and entrepreneurs themselves to recognise the need for and seek out relevant support. One example of the way a government can shape the environment rather than mandate the advice is the tax breaks implemented September 2013 to encourage employee shareholding. Organisations that want to take advantage of the new environment may well need to ask how to do it, creating demand for professional advice.

Beyond fostering an environment in which the need for good advice is acknowledged, Jesse suggests the other key point is to watch for the successful models to emerge and support them as they do – rather than mandate how and where social enterprises should exist. While there are many people within the sector who believe in the benefits of alternative forms of enterprise, like co-ops or employee-owned businesses, his concern is that people outside the sector, notably in HM Treasury, sometimes suggest that if social enterprise models worked, there'd be more of them already. For this reason, he thinks only successful, large-scale models will help bring about change. He acknowledges that waiting for these models to "break out" is a "long-term thing, not something for a single political cycle".

It is a source of some frustration to Jesse that even though the UK was the country that invented co-ops, there are, in relative terms, far fewer of them in the UK than in European countries, or indeed the US. Through chairing the All Party Parliamentary Group on Employee Ownership, Jesse is attempting to raise awareness of the benefits of this type of employee involvement in organisations as part of a move to encourage more of it in the future.

Jesse's future vision of social enterprises is of organisations that work for all stakeholders involved. For business itself, he suggests that good social enterprise management can mean practices almost identical to those celebrated in large emerging technology companies, as they embody ideas of high entrepreneurialism, but deliver it through a flatter hierarchy. He also suggests that social enterprises often have a lot of human capital but little financial investment, so "they tend to be quite entrepreneurial because they have to hustle and can't just rely on a large capital surplus". With the caveat that good governance has to be in place to moderate the potential for internal politics to disrupt the entrepreneurial spirit of the organisation, Jesse thinks that these types of approaches will help the sector expand in a mixed economy.

Going beyond the business and looking at the people it affects, Jesse's vision of the future, involving employee ownership, is one where employees are more fulfilled and happy to work effectively. He thinks this will come about if they work in an environment of mutual respect promoted by greater involvement. Finally, he thinks businesses run in this way, particularly service providers, will be valued for their human touch. This potential future is, therefore, very much focused on what the economy can do for human beings, rather than just the other way around.

About Jesse Norman MP

Jesse Norman has been the Conservative Member of Parliament for Hereford and South Herefordshire since 2010, and during that time has been a member of the Treasury Select Committee. He has also chaired the All-Party Parliamentary Group on Employee Ownership.

With a BA from Oxford University and an MPhil and PhD from University College London, Jesse has had a varied career including running an educational project in Eastern Europe, working for BZW (part of Barclays) and teaching philosophy at University College London and Birkbeck. He is a member of Council at the National Institute for Economic and Social Research. He has also been involved in a wide variety of voluntary and charitable work.

As a writer, Jesse's credits include *Compassionate Conservatism*, *Compassionate Economics*, *The Big Society*, *The Case for Real Capitalism* and *Edmund Burke: Politician, Philosopher, Prophet* – as well as many print articles.

JIM BROWN
Beyond a 'sense' of ownership

'To run an enterprise you need the support of all
stakeholders to create wealth.'

"There is a widespread belief that you cannot invest **equity** in social enterprises," Jim Brown explains. He's just spent the start of our interview telling me about his career trajectory as researcher, advisor, practitioner and consultant in the co-operative, social enterprise and social investment movements for over 30 years. When he describes how he moved from focusing on the experience of people at work, to who owns and controls where they work and on to who invests in those work organisations, the progression seems straightforward. Yet, some of his more recent work on equity investment in social enterprises and also around the regulation of **community share issues** has entered areas that some in the social enterprise and co-operative movement are not always comfortable with.

"To run an enterprise you need the support of all stakeholders to create wealth," says Jim. But he highlights how in various different models of business, rather than acknowledging this need for all-round support, one type of stakeholder is privileged over others – whether it be the shareholders in mainstream profit-distributing businesses or the workers in a traditional worker co-op. Yet in the current business environment, he says, people are coming to understand how people involved in businesses might occupy more than one traditional role within the business (worker, owner, customer, supplier, investor).

"You hear a lot of talk about giving people a 'sense of ownership'. Well I say that's a poor relation to real ownership, that is to say legal title." Jim's experience advising social enterprises underlines for him the importance of engaging with the ideas of investment and ownership rather than taking pre-existing approaches for granted. It also leads him to believe that tackling law and regulation is necessary for facilitating future alternative approaches to creating wealth for diverse types and groups of people, including more recognition of "common wealth – wealth created in common that remains our common property".

Jim defines social enterprises by legal form as Community Interest Companies, charities that trade or Industrial and Provident Societies on the grounds that defining what is and what is not a social enterprise is absolutely necessary if policy and regulation is to be developed. "HMRC can't give tax relief to something indefinable," says Jim, highlighting the consultation launched in July 2013 by the government on social investment tax relief. It's also important for his work on the *Community Shares Handbook* that the law defines what organisations people are investing in and on what terms. "There are now over 500 community share initiatives around the country and the vast majority of these have been established in the last five years." They mark a different way of approaching investment to that of conventional transferable shares – shares which the owner is free to sell to whom they want at the price the buyer will accept. The problem with this as an approach is that "It's a speculative price – the seller's always going to have trouble defining value, look at the [sell-off] of Royal Mail. Ownership becomes about speculation and it's all in the interest of the investors, not the organisation."

The alternative approach in Industrial and Provident Societies is shares that are not transferable, but are withdrawable if you want to end your ownership: "The company has to buy back your share plus any historic added-value in the form of interest payments. So the actual added value created by the organisation is added to your share account. It's not speculation." The difference is therefore that the owners are interested in the organisation, in the longer-term value of their shares and their involvement in how the organisation is run – rather than just their speculative profit.

It's a fascinating approach and one that Jim sees as pro-enterprise, at the same time as reflecting a desire to see capitalism to some extent reformed: "Capitalism is not responding well to the challenges of sustainability. New ways of running an enterprise economy are needed," Jim explains. In providing alternative approaches to investment, he expects "shifts in how we understand things. We aren't providing a replacement regime but giving people the opportunity to do things like run community pubs and shops that make sense to them." For Jim, it is most likely that the co-operative, social enterprise and social investment movements will play their part in the development of the wider economy through diffusion of ideas rather than any large-scale shift towards whole-scale adoption of their approaches. "What's always stood out for me is how the co-operative and social enterprise sector has been a microcosm of the larger picture, working through issues in the wider society. Its contribution is that people can work towards [these alternatives] and it provides a space to explore possibilities."

This exploration has not always gone smoothly and he wonders how it will develop and change in the future. Jim describes how social enterprises were "a pet project of government in the early 2000s. But the public spending cuts since 2010 have had a major impact on the social enterprise sector." The reduction in funding also meant that existing advisors and specialists in social enterprise found it hard to continue supporting alternative ways of doing business – although he thinks the most effective and committed of them find a way to make a living at it and supporting the future evolution of the movement, whatever happens.

Looking to the future, Jim's hope for social enterprise is simple: "Hopefully there will be a much more ready acceptance where people say, 'Why wouldn't a shop be locally owned?'" Through all his legal, regulatory and advisory work to foster and enable community ownership, it's all ultimately about normalisation. "It's about making [alternative types of ownership] part and parcel of what you anticipate and changing people's expectations of where their money is."

About Jim Brown

Jim Brown is the strategic adviser to the Community Shares Unit, a UK government-funded initiative to promote and develop good practice in community investment. The unit was created in October 2012, following a successful action-research programme for the UK Prime Minister's

Cabinet Office, launched in 2009, for which Jim was the lead consultant. Since then, more than 100 communities across the UK have raised over £15 million in equity finance for community ventures such as food stores, pubs, football clubs, renewable energy schemes, community workspaces, bookshops, community farms and fair trade initiatives.

Community shares use a unique form of equity, called withdrawable share capital, enshrined in a body of corporate legislation for co-operatives and community benefit societies. In May 2013 the unit launched an equity crowd-funding website dedicated exclusively to community shares. Jim Brown wrote regulatory guidance material for the *Community Shares Handbook*, which was overseen by HM Treasury, the newly formed Financial Conduct Authority and the Charity Commission. The Community Shares Unit is based at Co-operatives UK, the national federal body for co-operatives.

Jim Brown has written extensively on community investment, as the commissioning editor of *Co-operative Capital* and author of *Community Investment using IPS legislation* and *The Practitioners' Guide to Community Shares* as well as in articles for the *Guardian* newspaper, the *Social Enterprise Journal*, and the *Journal of Co-operative Studies*; he is also on its Editorial Advisory Board. He has held visiting research fellowships at the University of Bristol, the University of East London and the University of Wollongong in Australia, where he was the winner of the Commonwealth Relations Trust scholarship.

Interacting with national and local government

One of the major controversies of social enterprise is how close it gets to national and local government and with what consequences. Some see social enterprises as the more democratic, local and effective alternative to centrally-organised public services, while others fear that well intentioned adoption of social enterprise models could in the end lead to 'privatisation by the back door'. These pieces comment on the role of national and local government both as enablers and barriers to quality social enterprise service delivery.

Dick Newby compares the social enterprise movement to the women's liberation movement by suggesting that a legal framework that enables social enterprises is important, but only hard work, pioneers and good examples within that framework will actually bring about cultural changes in the way businesses are expected and allowed to operate.

Voicing the concerns of many other interviewees in this book, Anna Whitty explains why local authorities need to start thinking in a more joined-up way to really open up opportunities for social enterprises to improve services.

Preventative, long-term, locally relevant work is required to make the difference to people's lives, but that doesn't always fit in with local government agendas, says Graham Wiles.

Mark Sesnan suggests that the complex task of procuring public services needs attention and that good education for commissioners and procurement officers is what is required.

Steve Mollison explores why big businesses and the public sector currently seem to find it hard to trust social enterprises.

Simon Watson highlights the role small, well-run, local social enterprises could have in providing more accountable public services – but cautions that it would be easy for new public service management methods to pay lip service to ideals of engagement and empowerment rather than guarantee them in practice.

LORD NEWBY
Quality services flow from the right ethos

'The first legal foundations are there. So it's time for social enterprises to show what they are made of.'

According to Dick Newby, The Lord Newby OBE, social enterprises are "organisations that seek to deliver goods and services using commercial disciplines, but with a social rather than a purely profit purpose". As the peer who sponsored the **Social Value Act** through the Lords and the co-founder of a social enterprise called Sport for Life International, he has spent some time thinking about what the appropriate nature and role of these "commercial disciplines" in social enterprise might be, from both a policy and practical perspective: "A social enterprise has got to realise that you've got to deliver a surplus in order to survive and grow. And the fact that you don't distribute that surplus is what makes it a social enterprise. But equally, the fact that you've got to have a surplus is a defining attitude in how you make the thing operate."

Throughout the interview Dick returns to the central idea that social enterprises are distinctive from organisations in other sectors because of their attitude and ethos. Of course, this leaves the door open for his definition to include multiple and diverse types and sources of social enterprise: "There won't be one source of energy or inspiration or people who do it. It'll develop in a whole raft of ways, which at the moment you can't entirely predict." Given the current initiatives and direction of travel, he anticipates, for example church buildings and resources providing incubation space for social enterprises, spin-outs from the NHS, local government and universities as well as organisations led by inspired and motivated individuals.

While Dick Newby sees many different kinds of social enterprise as being possible, he is particularly interested in what the sector "can do in respect of public service delivery" in the future. Even though using 'commercial disciplines' within public services may have become more common over the last 20 years, he thinks that good social enterprises outperform other sectors both on price and quality. However, there are still some people in national and local government, who worry that social enterprises aren't up to the job. "The worry that people have at the moment is that social enterprises are too flaky, they're small, they're under-capitalised, they haven't got much of a track record and they're run by people with beards and sandals, that sort of thing. So that's the challenge." He compares the movement towards social enterprise as having parallels with a lot of movements, for instance the women's movement in the second half of the twentieth century: "You've got to have the legal underpinning to allow you to do it [promote women in business/ promote social enterprises], but the law won't do it on its own...In the nicest possible way, they've got to be pushy, because otherwise it won't happen." Just as women had to assert their rights and go for opportunities, the law had to allow their progression and protect them against discrimination.

The Social Value Act was an attempt to provide the legal side of that movement for social enterprises. "The hope with the Social Value Act is that we can get more services which the state provides, provided by social enterprises." Of course, this type of commissioning had been possible, although not commonly practised, before the Social Value Act was conceived. It therefore seemed important to ask Dick why new legislation was necessary. "This will get me into terrible trouble, but most people who work in procurement aren't hugely imaginative, they're risk averse because the incentives for them as individuals are not to cock up," he explains, adding "what the Social Value act seeks to do is to slightly redress the balance so that people are being encouraged to think a bit more widely about who they look to procure." He talks of the Social Value Act as like dropping "a little depth charge" under complacency in procurement by making it a legal requirement to think about social value when they buy.

On the other side of the movement, Dick thinks that the state of the social enterprise sector in 20 years' time will rest on the type of proof today's social enterprises provide of their quality and ability to deliver, just as pioneering women proved themselves in business in the face of prejudice and barriers and silenced their detractors. "I would hope that social enterprises do become very much part of the mainstream, or a bigger part of the mainstream," he muses, "but it won't happen automatically, they're going to have to prove their worth at every point and demonstrate to decision-makers that they can deliver better value for money and better quality." Without this proof, the legal underpinning is just that – a foundation without a building upon it.

Dick hopes that, in 20 years' time, social enterprises will have built on that foundation and claimed their place in the mainstream to improve the quality of life for people in the UK needing health and welfare services. Of course, he is drawn to social enterprises partly because he thinks the services they provide will be better value for the government than other options, for instance when they are more cost-efficient in the way they pay their employees than other sectors and because they don't have to distribute profit to external shareholders. However, he returns throughout to the idea that the crucial difference social enterprise can provide is the ethos of organisations that are built around the idea of operating with the idea of consumer welfare at their core, and who only employ people who are serving that mission. "People who are providing services – it's not just technical ability. It's the way they do it…And, arguably, good social enterprises are better than anybody else…because of the motivation of the people." For Dick, then, quality services and therefore social value flow from the right ethos. He thinks that "The first legal foundations are there. So, it's time for social enterprises to show what they are made of."

About The Lord Newby OBE

Dick Newby is a life peer and is the Liberal Democrat Chief Whip, Government Deputy Chief and Treasury Spokesman in the House of Lords. He was founder and co-chair of the All-Party Parliamentary Group on Social Enterprise and sponsored the Public Services (Social

Value) Act 2012 in the House of Lords. He is also Patron for Sport for Life International.

Dick founded Sport for Life International with Jane Power as a social enterprise to deliver educational opportunities linked to sport – principally cricket. This followed pioneering work with The Prince's Trust on linking the Trust's work with young people with professional football and cricket clubs. Sport for Life international has established education centres in the Test Match cricket grounds in Barbados, St Lucia, St Vincent and Trinidad, and ran a similar programme in Mirpur, Pakistan. The centres include an IT suite and combine academic work with developing the interpersonal, communications and leadership skills which come from playing a team sport. In the UK, the organisation works with inner city communities, in Birmingham and London, using cricket as a personal development tool for primary- and secondary-age boys and girls.

ANNA WHITTY
The social enterprise sector needs honest self-appraisal

'A successful social enterprise leader needs to put in the effort – the hours I do now are no different from the corporate world.'

"It's crucial for social enterprises to stand back and be honest about their strengths as well as their weaknesses," says Anna Whitty, chief executive at ECT Charity which represents the ECT group of companies that provide community transport services in West London, Milton Keynes, West Cheshire and Dorset. She's talking about how the silver lining of a business setback that happened a number of years ago, compelled the organisation to re-evaluate its existing position – "it made us go back to our roots and to pursue a clearly defined social mission".

ECT – originally Ealing Community Transport – used to run multiple ventures which included recycling furniture and paint, kerbside waste management and a railway business alongside its bus and door-to-door services. When the economic downturn hit, ECT's borrowing facility was withdrawn which meant that ECT had to sell its waste management and railway businesses. The sale attracted a great deal of press attention due to the fact that a large and prominent social enterprise was involved. As a consequence of the sale, ECT stood back and reassessed its core purpose: "Our mission was (and still is) to provide transport for the local community including people with mobility difficulties who find it hard to access mainstream transport. The consolidation of our activities was one of the best things that could have happened as it meant that we were once again true to our social mission." ECT Charity is now the umbrella brand for various community transport operations across the UK and Anna says: "We're proud to be both a charity and a social enterprise at the same time. Our overarching aim is to reduce isolation by getting people out of their homes and participating in their local community."

For Anna, the key to maintaining a successful and sustainable business is an honest appraisal of the organisation and its staff, as well as oneself: "When I was promoted from operations director to CEO, I knew that I had a steep learning curve ahead of me. Crucially, however, I knew how the business functioned at an operational level, and was also able to learn from ECT's past mistakes. Social enterprises are at risk of becoming so preoccupied with achieving their social mission that they forget to stand back and conduct regular and honest self-assessments." Anna is clear that a key element for an organisation's success is good leadership together with an appropriately skilled team to deal with management, governance and operational issues: "Recognising your employees' strengths and weaknesses is crucial in developing an effective team – but this doesn't happen overnight, personal development takes time."

Looking to the future, Anna does not think that capacity-building initiatives are always the answer to helping social enterprises start up and grow. Rather, she says: "There's plenty of easily obtainable and free information available, you just need to be willing to invest time and energy in learning from it." This ties in with Anna's view on the idea of honest appraisal – social enterprise leaders must be honest about their limitations and be proactive in addressing them: "A successful social enterprise leader needs to put in the effort – the hours I do now are no different from the corporate world. Successful social enterprises and charities shouldn't be any less professional or efficient than a traditional business, and they shouldn't expect hand-outs – if they require consultancy or a professional's time, they should pay for it." Anna's vision is that social enterprises will be staffed by teams that actively develop their organisations in realistic ways and recognise the need to invest in that process.

Anna's vision extends to social enterprise infrastructure organisations – she hopes that they too conduct honest self-appraisals and recognise that they have a strategic and forward-looking role, rather than simply a remedial one. "If you look at the Community Transport

Association, some members believe that they are simply there to support failing community transport organisations," Anna explains, "but I don't think that that's their only purpose. Rather, they should also play a strategic role by keeping the community transport message current and engaging with all stakeholders and decision-makers."

This kind of profile-raising is necessary if community transport organisations are to thrive in the future, according to Anna: "Speak to anybody in local authorities and they'll say that 'transport is always a problem' in that the services are insufficient and inefficient. However, the problem doesn't lie with the transport itself per se, rather, there is an unwillingness to pay for it. This issue is compounded by the fact that local government considers transport by dividing it into 'silos', for example, transport in education, transport in social services and so on." Each of these departments have their own budgets and commercial contracts to deliver their specific transport services and they don't talk to each other and collaborate. For instance, currently you have one bus to take children to school in the morning and then it sits empty all day until the afternoon school-run, and another bus which delivers people to hospital appointments and waits until the bus is full before leaving for the return journey. In contrast, Anna says, "My vision for the future is for collaboration between local government departments and an integrated approach to transport. So, instead of having buses standing empty for half the day, you could take children to school in the morning, then while they're at school that bus might run door-to-door journeys for older people to enable them to get out of the house and reduce their isolation."

In line with the thread that has run all of the way through our interview, Anna believes that an honest and pragmatic realism is needed. Getting the right people within local authorities talking to each other and developing ways of procuring for social value, is going to be a long and drawn-out process: "I will just keep chipping away at this, and I hope others will too. It's a difficult process, but I'm passionate about delivering our social value, and that's what motivates me to keep going."

About Anna Whitty

Anna graduated from the University of London with a degree in mathematics and went on to join British Airways on a graduate management training scheme. Anna spent four years at British Airways working in a fast-paced operational environment, and after a career break, moved into the charity sector. Anna joined ECT Charity in 1989 and gained extensive experience in passenger transport and operational management. She rose to operations director and was then appointed as CEO in June 2008. Since becoming CEO, Anna has stabilised the organisation, clarified its vision, refreshed the brand and recruited a new board. She also oversaw the expansion of the business from Ealing to include operations in Milton Keynes, Cheshire and Dorset.

Last year, Anna led ECT Charity's ground-breaking partnership with 24 community transport operators (many of whom were also social enterprises) across the country to provide the Accessible Shuttles service for the London 2012 Olympic and Paralympic Games. Mayor of London Boris Johnson hailed the team "the unsung heroes" of London 2012 and noted that, "The community transport sector, under ECT Charity's leadership, demonstrated what first class accessible transport should look like."

About ECT Charity

ECT Charity is a leading charity in the UK which provides high quality, safe, accessible and affordable transport for the communities it serves, thereby increasing community engagement and participation and improving the quality of people's lives. It is a charity and a social enterprise that uses high-calibre staff to deliver transport solutions to people who need assistance with their mobility, to community groups and to transport commissioners.

The transport solutions provided by ECT Charity have been developed to cover a specifically identified and unmet local transport need. Its target market comprises those people who cannot use mainstream public transport due to mobility or other difficulties, or because ordinary public transport or other services have been withdrawn from their area. Thus, ECT Charity's community transport services for local communities delivers a public benefit by supporting participation, engagement and enabling people to have more opportunities in their lives

The community transport services provided by ECT Charity include transport for groups, individual door-to-door services, home-to-school transport and local buses.

ECT Charity has strong partnerships with local authorities and other public bodies in different parts of the UK, as well as other partners – adding value to their services with a focus on quality, community benefit and expertise in the field of accessible transport.

In 2012, ECT Charity delivered, as lead partner, the London 2012 Accessible Shuttles project on behalf of the Olympic Delivery Authority. This large-scale, complex project was recognised as one of the outstanding transport successes of the London 2012 Olympic and Paralympic Games and positioned accessible transport at the heart of future Olympic planning. The success of this project not only placed the provision of accessible transport high on the agenda of transport providers, but also provided a platform from which ECT Charity was able to demonstrate the professionalism and capacity of the community transport sector as a whole, and of ECT Charity specifically.

GRAHAM WILES
Demonstrating the circular economy

'... and then we built a mini fish farm on a double decker bus.'

Fish farms, floating cafes, historic railway carriages, self-build housing; there is no end to the ideas and stories that flow out of Graham Wiles who runs the Green Business Network in Yorkshire. Although the business ideas might be diverse, what unites them is Graham's passion for creating opportunities that provide long term support for marginalised people in economically and environmentally sustainable social enterprises.

Graham might be described as a serial social entrepreneur, although he is in fact, employed by Kirklees Council. He established the Able Project in Wakefield, raising sturgeon on a former landfill site, in the process creating jobs and training for young people with behavioural problems. He is now developing Able2, having been given a large piece of land by Kirklees Council that has a rich railway heritage which has spawned many ideas about reviving traditional craft industries and eventually a visitor centre.

Land and local heritage are crucial to the kinds of opportunities that Graham wants to create, developing a 'circular economy' approach. He explains that this is an enhancement of sustainable development and is a holistic approach that aims to tackle all aspects of the problems in society in an integrated way. He believes that this model provides a blueprint for how social enterprises should develop in future. Bringing into use neglected and low value pieces of land, creates opportunities for young people to develop their skills and confidence. One example he gives is the work they are doing to develop the current site.

"We're looking at dredging a lake on a nature reserve, and after blending clay with the dredged silt, we plan to make bricks ourselves, using techniques with low environmental impact and then we'll use the bricks to build a bird hide on the site." The young people working on the project gain skills and confidence that often takes them on to college.

Graham believes in local, low-tech approaches that minimise environmental impact, but says that it's a struggle to get others to understand. Although he researched some hi-tech approaches to pontoon building for floating homes in Holland, he says, "We didn't want a multi-million pound, high-tech project. We wanted to build with a cement mixer and a pair of hands attached to a low skilled person and that is what we are doing."

Graham believes that a key role for social enterprises is to "create opportunities for the most marginalised people in society, the people that no one else wants". The reason he thinks that this is a job for social enterprise is because in his experience this can take years. Working with prolific offenders with challenging behaviours takes years to make a lasting difference. "We create real jobs, it's not just helping them to write a CV," he says, referring to many mainstream, government-funded programmes. He describes their target group as reduced capacity workers, people who start as volunteers and trainees and who have often become permanent members of staff at Green Future Building, the social enterprise established to build the Able2 scheme, yet are still not capable of working at full capacity because of the range of problems they have.

"Lots of them are living in hostels; they need a home but can't get on the housing ladder. We need affordable housing and for that we need cheap land. So we are looking to develop a self-build housing project of floating homes, using land which is worthless to others."

Graham thinks that land ownership is critical to the growth of these kinds of social enterprises. "With publicly owned land we could do loads. Land is just sold; people don't appreciate what could be done with the country's assets." His frustration is deepened by his experience working across Europe in a network of more than 50 social enterprises. "Every single one of them is supported by the local authority or Central Government Funding. One partner in Poland has been given 200 acres of land and as it's a social enterprise, the land is still there for the benefit of the community, not shareholders. I can't understand why it doesn't happen in the UK."

One thing Graham thinks will have to change if social enterprises are to develop using these models is that the public sector must be more enabling. Having just had a two-year delay while awaiting the outcome of a planning application which had beneficial outcomes for the local community, but which was ultimately lost, he is sceptical about the ability of governments to think in the long term. "It takes a long time to turn people into survivors and there are no quick fixes and if you are working holistically with people, money needs to come from more than one budget. Social enterprises can be long term and strategic but government and local authorities are short term and budget driven." He sums up this problem. "We don't get money to keep people out of prison; only for stopping them going back [once they are in the system]. We were working with young offenders and all the money stopped as soon as they reached 18."

Ultimately, Graham thinks that there is massive potential for social enterprises to make lasting change in society. He wants to see more co-operative models, where social enterprises are owned by the people who work in them. He also thinks that greater recognition of social enterprises is needed and that this will be helped by more social and environmental accounting. Finally, he also wants to see more genuine partnership working with public authorities. "We need to recognise the true cost to society of the issues with which social enterprises work."

Graham is clear that the 'circular economy' approach of building sustainable, socially beneficial, long-term solutions to deep seated problems will ultimately save money for governments and society as a whole. Spending money ought to do two or three things at the same time. He thinks the potential is limitless.

"People laughed at us before but we've opened up more and more job opportunities. It is important that we keep within the limits of who we can help and that we keep the business sustainable because we can't rely on government grants. The activity must be worthwhile, we must create new jobs and they must be real jobs with potential for new industries in the UK. And we must make sure we are not displacing other jobs."And the fish farm on a bus? That was a project providing a learning resource in a school, re-using an old bus as a means of demonstrating biotechnology solutions and creating opportunities for young people to gain skills and ultimately get to college – that's the circular economy.

About Graham Wiles

Graham Wiles is an environmental science graduate with over 28 years' experience of working with people with complex needs, the last 18 of which he has managed the Green Business Network (GBN). He has worked in the private and public sectors as well as running his own successful company with experience gained both in the UK and Africa. It was while working in South Africa in the early 1980s that he began to focus on the principles of what is now known as the circular economy and recognised the potential benefits that could be achieved in relation to identifying solutions common to the environment, business and the community. He has established a number of social enterprises along the way as well as picking up a wide range of innovation awards.

About Green Business Network

Green Business Network (GBN) was established in 1995 as a support organisation to work with local small businesses, assisting them to reduce their environmental impacts and resource use. This service was soon expanded to include social enterprises as it was apparent that there were cases of symbiosis where a solution could be found that met the needs of both businesses and community. The latest of these has been Green Future Building Ltd (GFB) which is the delivery mechanism for GBN schemes and incorporates employment, training and real work experience for reduced capacity workers furthest away from the jobs market. It has social inclusion at its heart and has contracts with both the West Yorkshire Probation Trust and Kirklees Youth Offending Team for service delivery.

Although GFB was initially established to build a new aquaponics facility (the combination of fish farming and salad crop production), this quickly led to requests to replicate this facility on other sites throughout Yorkshire. GFB now has an impressive track record of successful completed projects under its belt and has picked up a number of high profile awards along the way.

MARK SESNAN

Putting entrepreneurial values into public services

'What limits our growth? The North Sea and the Atlantic Ocean.'

Mark Sesnan, the CEO of Greenwich Leisure Limited (GLL) has been doing this a long time. He has led the social enterprise for 20 years, from when it was first established and won the contract to run the leisure services for the London Borough of Greenwich. Prior to that he worked in local government, so he has a great deal of experience to draw on in our discussion, mostly focusing on the role of social enterprises delivering public services.

GLL has developed in many ways, now running leisure services in many other areas and, more recently, other public services. They have taken on the running of public library services and they have won contracts to run two major venues on the Olympic Park as part of the Olympic Legacy. Mark says that good social enterprise is about keeping the balance between four pillars: providing a good service, investing in good people, maintaining a positive community and environmental impact and running a sound and strong business, to be "the best at what we do. We are a people led organisation, that is not just about the HR, it's in our DNA. Our business grows to create more opportunities and to attract and keep the best people."

GLL is structured as a hybrid workers' co-op and stakeholder co-op. This means that each member of staff has one share that gives them one vote and they elect around half of the board from among their number. The other half of the board are stakeholders, partners and those with specialist skills. Even with over 6,000 employees, Mark says that there is still "a close alignment of the people who run the business and those who own it".

Mark sees the future of social enterprise as being linked very closely to the public sector and the delivery of good quality public services. Leisure services, he tells me, are now "a good mixed market with mature social enterprises competing with private providers and in-house provision. This enables local authorities to make choices about how they deliver services." Leisure services social enterprises are already part of the mainstream. "There are 120 leisure social enterprises in Britain. It's a lively market and lots of social enterprises are trying to get business but the drivers have changed significantly over the years." Mark points out that private providers have had to take on the social agenda that GLL and others have been delivering, so even if they don't win the business themselves, the social and community impact is much greater as a result of their strength in the market. "Social enterprises have improved the market; the private sector behaves better if social enterprises are in the market. It makes the competitive bit harder as everyone improves but we don't make special pleading."

Moving into the delivery of library services, though, has been very different and he sees GLL's methods as having the potential to improve the services on offer. "We get a cheque from the council to run the service, so we don't have to generate the money from our customers. Do you just hope that people will walk into the Library, or are there ways of generating income and improving the services? That's when you need a social entrepreneur to work with the librarians." Transferring staff from the public sector into a social enterprise is what can really make a difference to the service. Mark thinks that, increasingly, the environment in local authorities does not encourage people to do a good job. Working in a social enterprise "challenges them to perform, to shine and to do good".

The main barrier to social enterprises being able to fulfil their potential, however, is public sector procurement methods, where Mark says "there are a million challenges. Local authorities jumped into procurement without understanding it. The people who buy the paper clips were now being asked to commission complex public services." Mark is also critical of the advice that was often provided to procurement people, from some consultants who sell poor models of procurement practice. He admits that it is difficult to get right, but is concerned that these methods "may end up taking value out of the system, as often price becomes the only driver and this inevitably drives quality out."

Commissioning public services provides businesses such as GLL with great opportunities, but Mark thinks that procurement often gets in the way. In future, he thinks this is what needs to change. "Good procurement methods need to be taught and learned, developing schools of good practice. There needs to be feedback on what works and why. There should be much more focus on creating 'win–win' outcome focused partnerships rather than raw contracts." The other key danger for Mark is when social enterprise is presented as the solution for every problem. "Social enterprise is a way of doing business, and there's often an assumption we have the right to exist. You need the good ones, the ones with their heads screwed on, but there's a danger that the poor ones mess it up for everyone else." For this reason Mark sees GLL's role is "to do a good job and show people how to make it work, to be stable and to be bankable. The test is if social enterprises are still around in 20 years' time." GLL has a great platform to make its case with contracts to run the London Aquatic Centre and the Copper Box, a 6,000 seat arena on the Olympic site.

Mark says that he is not out to change the world, but he is concerned with "what we do today, tomorrow and the day after, to create better public services and that these services are better for the more disadvantaged".

Mark sees few limitations in the future for his own social enterprise or others' but he says it will be a long journey. "Our business", he says, "is a family of people who do good and work hard to be the best." In 20 years' time he wants GLL to be offering much more comprehensive services, geographically and thematically. As a mature social enterprise, this is a realistic vision for the organisation because, "We've been going for 20 years – we are looking forward to the next 20!"

About Mark Sesnan

Mark is managing director of GLL (Greenwich Leisure Limited), the pioneering staff-led charitable social enterprise that took over the operation of Greenwich Council's leisure centres in 1993 as an innovative 'spin out'.

GLL had a turnover of £5 million in 1993 with 150 employees operating seven leisure centres for one London Borough. Today GLL manages over 130 public leisure centres and libraries across England and has an annual turnover of around £131 million. GLL works with over 30 local councils, public agencies and sporting organisations and employs a diverse workforce of over 6,000 people. GLL is a mutual society and is owned by its members, all of whom are employees, and it is governed by a stakeholder board.

GLL played a key role in the 2012 London Olympic Games and today operates two of the key Olympic legacy venues: the Copper Box Arena, which opened to the public in July 2013 and the recently opened London Aquatics Centre.

GLL is the UK's largest charitable social enterprise in its field, delivering leisure, health and community services and libraries. Its mission is to provide high quality, accessible and affordable public services that are well used and contribute to the health, activity, social cohesion and education agendas.

Mark has worked with GLL from its formation in 1993 and was recognised as Ernst and Young's Social Entrepreneur of the Year in 2012. He currently holds the following positions:

- Member of the board of the Social Enterprise UK (SEUK)
- Honorary secretary of the Sports and Recreation Trusts Association (Sporta)
- Member of London Community Sports board
- Member of the SkillsActive board
- Member of GLL Sports Foundation board

About Greenwich Leisure Limited (GLL)

In 1993, Greenwich Council needed to find a new way to run its leisure centres because of public spending cuts and together with local stakeholders, they came up with a new model. The first of its kind in UK leisure, GLL was born. Seven centres were transferred to them, and success quickly followed. They created jobs and added new services to existing leisure centres. Since then, they've built lots of new facilities in the UK and their membership has gone from about 7,000 to nearly 450,000 with tens of millions of visitors every year. In 1996, they began expanding outside Greenwich and now run all kinds of community services and spaces across the UK.

GLL exist to make community services and spaces better for everyone. That means providing access to quality community leisure and fitness facilities – and more – at a price everyone can afford. They already manage over 115 facilities, and they're adding more all the time. They're a charitable social enterprise, which means that they work for the benefit of everyone: the public, the communities in which they work, the environment, their staff and their partners. As a result, they're proud to be the first leisure operator in the UK to be awarded both the Social Enterprise Mark and the Prime Minister's Big Society Award.

STEVE MOLLISON
Building trust in social enterprise

'It's about business first and foremost – if we're professional,
the trust will slowly get better.'

Steve Mollison, managing director of Graphic Design and Print
CIC, has a clear idea of what would improve opportunities for social
enterprises in the future, and it is grounded in his own experience.
As founder and manager of a CIC, Steve has seen the full range
of responses from customers, potential customers and financial
institutions to the idea of social enterprise. While some responses
are positive and helpful, in other cases he has not always been happy
about what he has heard. "When we tried to talk [to various public
sector agencies], one of the procurement officers said to us: 'We know
what you do, but we don't want to know,'" says Steve. "And finance
institutions – their eyes glaze over when you talk about it – they just
don't understand and don't want to understand."

Steve suggests that a lot of this reluctance to engage with the
idea of social enterprise is to do with trust. "It's not just that they
don't understand the message [that businesses can trade for a social
purpose], but they don't understand the skill base behind it as well,"
he says, because social enterprise involves more than traditional
business acumen, it requires it in combination with the capabilities
required to support vulnerable people. This combination may present
to those in financial institutions a set of people and motivations that
they are not used to encountering. According to Steve, an apparent
lack of willingness to seed-fund new ventures causes problems for

start-up social enterprises: "We don't just need support services, we do actually need a bit of cash as well. So many people have ideas that could help people, but you often hear, 'We could do X if only we had Y' and they can't get it."

According to Steve, this could easily be overcome if large businesses and institutions responded to their community responsibilities in good faith, rather than through what he sees as cynical marketing opportunities – "I would hope that in the future large organisations like banks could step out further in their usual work and have a mandate to help social enterprises, not just to send out staff members one day a year to do something for charities."

He also gives an example of where he thinks large businesses pay lip service to social responsibilities, but will not take their engagement further: "We were approached to upload files to a large firm's intranet and we were only doing a few a month. We said to them, we want to do all of this work for you, let us do more, but they immediately said "No", that as a social enterprise we were 'high risk'. But I think we're low risk considering the dedication we put into running this business and the reason for it." Steve suggested the business in question had perhaps found it useful to have had minimal engagement with a social enterprise when they were bidding for contracts with councils and other public sector agencies. Just as in the environmental sector where the term 'green-washing' explains organisations making a show of being environmental to gain benefits, he sees similar things happening when mainstream organisations engage with the social enterprise sector in minimal ways.

It seems, then, that trust is vital in both directions in social enterprise relationships and that as a new and alternative model, social enterprise is not yet adequately understood or accepted for that trust to be widespread. For that reason, Steve suggests, social enterprises have to be smarter in getting to grips with their perceived disadvantages: "We are naturally at a disadvantage because there's a sort of brinksmanship with our money – it'd be easy to go over one way to business priorities or the other to social priorities." To manage this potential for imbalance, Steve suggests that strategic planning is an absolute must. "It's about business first and foremost – if we're professional, the trust will slowly get better," he predicts. Yet he thinks this would be helped along by people who are trusted already shouting louder about the potential of social enterprises: "It would be good to have a business-oriented social enterprise champion telling the City [of London] and others about what we do."In this same vein, he also favours the inclusion on social enterprise boards of suitable directors who have mainstream business experience, to make sure uncomfortable truths are spoken: "We've had a person join our board who owns a corporation. He's purely there for business advice – blunt, kick-up-the-arse-type business advice. It'd be great if business people with a wealth of experience could support up and coming social enterprises."

In 20 years, Steve hopes that Graphic Design and Print will have grown and become an enterprise centre, not only providing opportunities for people who face disadvantage as it does now, but also providing inspiration for other potential social enterprises. He'd like to be working in a context where social enterprise has become part of everyday life for many in the community, where social enterprises give emotional and pastoral support as a matter of course as part of and alongside more formal training and employment opportunities.

He also hopes that the public sector will recognise the benefit of social enterprises and not use their size and economic power to compete with them. He worries about this power extending to wholly-owned subsidiary organisations of public sector bodies. This reflects the increasing number of businesses that are externalised public services, still contracted to the public authority of which they used to be a part. These organisations sit in a slightly undefined position between public and private sector ways of operating. Steve is concerned that they operate without the independence (and therefore risk in the market) that social enterprises have and therefore there is not the even playing field for social enterprises that Steve believes could provide better services.

"What I would like in the future is for government to make it mandatory to engage with social enterprises, discuss what we do and consider what we could contribute – understand we're going further than councils ever can do. I went to Westminster to discuss the **Social Value Act** and at that time our concern was that procurement officers would ignore this new law. I've just sent 36 booklets around the Eastern Region asking them to engage with this law and I've had absolutely no reply," Steve explains. He hopes that this lack of engagement will be overcome so that in 20 years, "a lot of people that are finding life difficult will be better off. I hope we'll have reached a level [of support provision] where people could be helped a lot quicker than they are today and that change could take place, especially in the poorer or more disadvantaged parts of the community."

About Steve Mollison and Graphic Design and Print CIC

Steve is co-founder and managing director of Graphic Design and Print CIC. Graphic Design and Print CIC was set up to benefit people who are disadvantaged or socially excluded. They employ people from the community, provide NVQs and offer training. The company is registered with the UK Register of Learning Providers.

Both founding directors have a commitment to social inclusion and equality of opportunity which has instilled an interest in looking for new ideas and innovative solutions in developing a community where everyone enjoys the benefits of prosperity, and where everyone has chances to work and to learn.

Graphic Design and Print CIC believes people with learning disabilities are citizens first and foremost, and public services, together with the private sector, need to respond appropriately. This means that the responsibility to ensure all people can enter the workforce is a community-based responsibility not one simply for health and social care.

Individuals are offered real life chances, with paid employment and the experience to work for a company that is commercially focused. Other benefits include a chance of independence, inclusion into the wider community and choice in daily life. Graphic Design and Print CIC ensures people work within an environment that is safe, providing an anti-oppressive workplace, having respect for all, and a commitment to empower people to reach their full potential.

SIMON WATSON
People power makes the difference

'People care about what they're doing, the services they provide and the impact on users. This is a huge resource and we can make the most of it.'

Simon Watson is Unison's National Officer for the Community and Voluntary Sector, the representative of the public sector union's links with social enterprises. Some social enterprise staff are members of Unison and as social enterprises take on public services, Simon and his colleagues are increasingly having to think about what that means. Simon is clear that there are real benefits to service users provided by social enterprises – but on condition that they are delivered by small community groups or organisations where front line staff are in control. "If the workforce is involved in the governance and how [the social enterprise] operates, it can be a better way of providing public services – people on the front line see how things work and don't work." His worry is that bigger social enterprises are just chasing contracts and end up behaving no differently to existing public authorities or private sector contractors.

The main theme that we keep coming back to is accountability. Simon believes that this is the key factor that makes services better. He reminds us that public sector organisations will always retain democratic accountability for public services, but as the links between these organisations and the providers commissioned to deliver services are changing, it is vital to make sure accountability is in the mix.

Public services can be delivered under contract by private sector companies, traditional charities or social enterprises. Often the staff involved have been transferred to the contractor from a previous contractor or the local authority. "The public may not notice [the difference in services supplied by a social enterprise or a public sector organisation] if the same people are emptying their bins, but there is a difference. People who are elected have accountability but so do small social enterprises, delivering services in their local community." As local councils have elected councillors who are ultimately responsible for the work that they do, many social enterprises have members who live in the local communities so that local people can still influence how services are delivered. Simon's preference is for services to be delivered by these small organisations but also acknowledges that "larger scale social enterprises need a formal democratic framework to keep the accountability...it's important to have the ethos of staying close to your roots and not just chasing new opportunities elsewhere."

The big problem is when outsourcing is being done in order to save money or to "get someone else to do the dirty work" of making cuts and reorganising services. He is also concerned about workforce issues, such as wage levels and job security in larger social enterprises, when they are competing for contracts that are often awarded on the basis of the lowest price. "Sometimes strong social goals mean that the organisation can overlook the conditions of the workforce. There needs to be a strong moral compass, which is undermined if staff are not treated well. Part and parcel of the social goal is that the staff are treated well."

Following on from our discussion about accountability, Simon, not surprisingly, thinks that there are two ways that social enterprises can be set up. One is by setting up small social enterprises grown out of community activism "that meet the community's needs. I want to see these organisations mobilising existing 'community capital' to achieve their goals around, for example, recycling, advice-giving and childcare – that's where the real added value is." The other is the co-operative model, again focusing on accountability. "Co-ops are interesting," he says, "they've got lots to give the sector. The new models of public service mutuals that involve the workforce are being promoted very heavily. But there is an issue about accountability – if they are owned by the staff, how are they democratically accountable to the wider community?"

Simon recognises that in the public sector when money is tight, the disadvantages of large and unwieldy organisations that are slow to change can be seen. "People in public services are not always given opportunities to innovate. Smaller organisations are good at this." However, he recognises that while these small organisations can be well organised when they start up because the people involved know each other and can find ways to resolve any issues, "they need more formal ways of resolving things as they get bigger. Yesterday I was dealing with an issue about disability discrimination, people wanted to know what was good practice. Recently we've had issues relating to violence and aggression in the workplace. People at work are under stress because of the demands placed on them and the people they are trying to help are under more stress because their money is tight and this can lead to aggressive behaviour and bullying. In some cases organisations are trying to deliver the same quality of contract for less money and this puts people under pressure. Staff need experienced support from unions or HR departments."

Simon comes up with one unusual perspective on the relationship between public sector organisations and social enterprises. "Social enterprises need to make a surplus but they need to have the guts to put that at risk because of the ethos of the organisation." He sees this risk as a consequence of innovative and socially committed organisations delivering services that people need. The role of the public sector would then be to act as a back-up, "if social enterprises are seen as being of value in the local area, they can be supported by local authorities, conditional on them staying small and close to their roots".

The real value of small social enterprises, according to Simon, is that in communities where people have traditionally felt that they have no influence over how services are delivered, they are "stepping into the vacuum. It's important because they give people the experience of making decisions, this gives individuals more control over their lives, if they want to make a difference, they can – it creates real empowerment."

He concludes by saying that "personal relationships are important, you know who in the community needs help. It's more efficient because it's based on networks of people and you get really rapid feedback, not just management statistics. It's like our trade union activists really, they know their members and can sort out problems on the ground before they become formal – it's much more efficient."

About Simon Watson

Simon Watson is the National Officer (Community and Voluntary Sector) at UNISON. Having been a teacher and then database analyst, Simon joined UNISON as a researcher in 2002 before taking over service delivery issues and procurement in local government. He then moved to the community and voluntary sector, developing policy and leading negotiations with national not-for-profit employers. Outside of paid work, he has established a housing co-operative and participated in many varied grassroots community organisations.

About Unison

UNISON represents and acts for members working in a range of public services and utilities, whether they're employed by private companies, public authorities or in the community and voluntary sector. They represent members, negotiate and bargain on their behalf, campaign for better working conditions and pay and for public services.

Awareness, survival and resources

Businesses need money and people to operate – but to some, the alternative nature of the social enterprise model can make it seem a risky place to invest time and money. The following pieces show why a lack of awareness or understanding can put up barriers to gaining opportunities, appropriate staff or resources and how the way forward will involve thinking how to overcome these barriers.

Claire Dove highlights the role of infrastructure organisations like Social Enterprise UK in providing a voice for the sector.

Mandy Young found it useful to find out that her initiative was a social enterprise and points out the gap in business education in schools – where private profit is often the only reason given for setting up a business.

Start-up is key. Malcom Hayday explains how he wants to see support for people moving from an idea to setting it up in reality and more appropriate avenues for financing those ideas.

Local people can run things effectively too, says Steve Wyler, concerned that genuinely involving and placing power with local people can be seen by some as a hindrance, rather than a help to social enterprises.

Guy Turnbull highlights the difficulty of conveying the idea of mutual benefit: that someone winning doesn't have to be at the cost of someone else losing.

Thinking like an eight-year old (that is to say not always going for what seems to be the 'obvious' or 'traditional' approach) is a distinct benefit, in the eyes of Chris Dabbs, who wants social enterprises to raise awareness of innovative new ways to improve people's lives.

Sally Reynolds reminds us that social enterprises do not have an automatic right to survive, but that we should be pushing for the highest quality and best run organisations to thrive and the others to change or perish.

CLAIRE DOVE
Hoping for growth grounded in values

'Everything we do has a set of values at the heart.'

As CEO of flourishing social enterprise Blackburne House and chair of Social Enterprise UK, Claire Dove switches easily between thinking about the practicalities of carrying out business at a local level and the needs of the sector at national level. Her hope for the future both locally and nationally is simple: growth.

"From the point of view of our social enterprise, [the plan for the future] really is to grow and consolidate the businesses, always remembering…that providing women's education is of paramount importance," says Claire. "We do our education through our social enterprises," she explains, describing how the social and commercial goals of the organisation mesh. While the purpose of Blackburne House is to provide educational opportunities to women, the social enterprises supporting that purpose are many and varied, including a café, conference facilities, a health and fitness spa and a construction academy providing training and progression opportunities to tradeswomen. It's all part of building a strong social economy. The entrepreneurial variety of these ventures illustrates Claire's enthusiasm for finding business-embedded solutions, rather than tweaking the edges of traditional charitable work: "We have to be careful it's not a charity just selling a few things – it is a business model, the difference from traditional business models is that there is no shareholder value."

This new model is an approach Blackburne House has taken from the start, although Claire reminds me that when she started out: "it was before people used the words 'social enterprise'". The key for Claire and her colleagues in the beginning (and her tip for the future for other social enterprises) was to recognise that they not only needed to serve their students, but at the same time satisfy a wider range of customers who were the ones who could make or break the businesses. This involved keeping a clear view of the organisation's purpose and values, but also its revenue. "We have to be hard-nosed business people because we've got to survive," Claire explains. Sometimes this involves making hard decisions about the values that underpin the organisation, but Claire suggests that if these values are clear and well-articulated, they will provide a useful guide to the business and what is possible: "We're a value-driven organisation that stands by what we are. Values are integral to everything we do – recruitment, procurement…everything we do has a set of values at the heart."

One of the ways of gaining wider understanding of this value-based approach is to find a way to make the model more visible. Here's where Claire sees organisations like Social Enterprise UK making a difference: "We can't in our isolation just work in our own social enterprises. That's why Social Enterprise UK is so important – it's to get that message across." "We were aware that collectively, nationally, we needed a voice for these businesses," Claire continues. She sees this voice as useful for three key reasons that very much fit with her focus on getting the 'enterprise' part of social enterprise right. The first is around appropriate finance for social enterprises, the second is around opening up opportunities and the third is being a strong voice for the sector.

"One of the things we're very keen on is that there are appropriate levels of investment to grow your business," Claire explains. "One of the big things is that banks still do not support social enterprises in the way that they should. They need to lend to allow social enterprises to start up and grow – just like any other businesses. Within our sector we are growing financial institutions such as Big Society Capital and Big Invest and others, but they are relatively new and in their infancy." So one of the key things Claire would like to see in the future is a broader range of options for financing social enterprises as they both start up and grow.

Her second point is about the need to open up opportunities for social enterprises to move into new areas in the future, for instance public services: "I think the **Social Value Act** is imperative at this time of austerity, we need to know that the money being spent [by the public sector] addresses the issues we face." Yet, while public services are one area of opportunity, Claire suggests growth in the sector should consist not just of deepened involvement in public services, but also expansion into areas that are currently still mostly the preserve of private businesses. "It's about widening the offer of social enterprises. For example, if someone dies in your family, you don't go shopping around, it's a time of great distress. So if you had an ethical funeral director, they could support people at that very difficult time." Claire's vision of the future therefore includes social enterprises across all areas of business.

Thirdly, while Claire is pushing for growth in the sector, she acknowledges that there are dangers lurking if the term gains greater public awareness: "What could subvert [the growth of the sector] is people taking on the brand of social enterprise for personal gain. That's the danger." This worry is not idle speculation. Social Enterprise UK and the movement as a whole lobbied in 2012 to stop a large US software company trademarking the term 'social enterprise' and won. Claire suggests the need for heightened awareness of how people are using the term will continue. While the instance in 2012 was a very visible attempt to appropriate the term, Claire points out that there are cases where the lines are blurred by organisations attempting to 'tick boxes' around providing social value, to further private gain. Although these could be a problem for the sector, she also holds out hope that even these first forays into addressing social value will bring private businesses closer to a social enterprise way of thinking: "I want the business sector to see the way we are and also to take on board the good practice we've put out there: getting added value out of contracts and providing environmental credentials, for instance."

Claire's hope for the future is to see a wide range of truly value-based social enterprises, big and small (just as in the private sector), run by a wide range of people "Social enterprises have demonstrated that they attract people from diverse backgrounds." She hopes that building a strong and vibrant social economy will influence the traditional business sector to adopt social enterprise values and philosophy. Ultimately, she thinks social enterprise growth lies in: "People who are entrepreneurial and have a passion for finding solutions."

About Claire Dove MBE

Claire Dove is CEO of award-winning social enterprise, Blackburne House. Under Claire's leadership, Blackburne House – one of the most successful women's organisations and social enterprises in the UK – grew and extended its reach into some of Liverpool's most disadvantaged areas, helping more than 1,000 people each year gain employment skills and training to support them into long-term work.

Claire believes that individuals are the catalyst for change and that social entrepreneurship is powerful driver in creating and sustaining positive social change. She therefore played a strategic role in bringing the first ever northwest-based School for Social Entrepreneurs to Blackburne House. The school provides training and ongoing opportunities to enable individuals to use their entrepreneurial and creative skills to develop social businesses to benefit their local communities.

Claire champions the social enterprise sector in her role as chair of Social Enterprise UK – the national body for social enterprise. She contributed to the development of the sector through her political and campaigns work – including her support for the Social Value Act, which became law in January 2013.

Claire was awarded an MBE for her work in the mid-1990s. She is also the recipient of an honorary fellowship of Liverpool John Moores University, a fellowship of the Royal Society of Arts, was voted nationally as an exemplary leader in Regeneration, is deputy lieutenant for Merseyside and a recipient of the Lifetime Achievement Award in the Queen's Award for Enterprise Promotion.

About Blackburne House

Blackburne House is a Grade II listed building, situated in Liverpool's famous Hope Street quarter, close to the city centre. It attracts thousands of visitors each year to facilities including a café bar, a women's health suite, conference facilities and a 30 place nursery.

It is home to a Beacon Status College which provides high quality adult and community education. The busy nursery, health suite, café bar and conference centre are all social businesses and the Blackburne House group also offers a business support service, a women's enterprise hub and a women's maintenance business.

Back in 1983, the Women's Technology and Education Centre (WTEC) was established. The organisation's aim was to attract low paid or unemployed women and equip them with the skills to progress into employment in technical professions; an area in which women are traditionally under-represented. By 1991 the organisation had expanded considerably and it was therefore necessary to find new accommodation. Over £4 million was raised in order to refurbish Blackburne House and provide a home for the educational and entrepreneurial activities that would provide opportunities for a diverse range of women.

The range of opportunities offered is important to those at Blackburne House, because they want to accommodate the many needs of women. Staff diagnose each individual's educational needs and tailor a programme to suit them. For this approach Blackburne House has repeatedly been awarded grade 1 status and been ranked in the top 10 per cent of educational providers in the country.

The organisation is driven by values, which are embedded in all they do. They want women to be inspired by their educational experience and to realise economic independence once they start their chosen careers. Many Blackburne House students overcome adversity and problems in their home lives with the support given to them as they work through their education. Claire Dove, the organisation's CEO states: "We are not just here to educate, we are here to listen, to support and to offer a place of safety and equality to women of all ages and backgrounds."

MANDY YOUNG
Education, capitalisation, replication

'Creating the Wembley of urban sport in Northamptonshire.'

Adrenaline Alley is a huge indoor urban centre catering for BMX, scootering, skateboarding and inline skating. Founder Mandy Young has built up the centre over the past decade from a small local project to a substantial charitable social enterprise. Yet she says "for me, it's never been about building a skate park". While this might seem an astonishing statement, given the success and prominence of Adrenaline Alley as an urban activities centre, she's making a point about the nature of social enterprise, where a business is not just a business, but is delivering on a social mission at the same time. "For me, it's been about channelling young people's enthusiasms in the right direction. The sports are the tools we use to engage young people and achieve other objectives," Mandy explains. So Adrenaline Alley now also provides all sorts of music, arts and media opportunities as well as its original urban sports activities: "We tap into sub-cultures to bring out other skills, not just riding skills."

Borne out of the distressing personal experience of her own son facing extreme anti-social behaviour when practising urban sports, Mandy started a small outdoor park to provide a safe environment for those who wanted to practice in Corby. But at the time "I didn't know it was a social enterprise," Mandy explains. She thought about making it a private business, but her ultimate goal was not personal gain, it was to benefit and create change for the young people in the community: "I thought – should I do this as a business? I could have put my house up [as security] and I could be pretty rich now. But this also wouldn't be what it is today." For Mandy, that type of attitude typifies those who start and develop social enterprises: "People running social enterprises are going the extra mile. They're not well paid but their personal experiences have been a benefit in running the business and providing the right outcomes."

It was only when Mandy gained the interest of and guidance from a range of support organisations, including Social Enterprise East Midlands, Business in the Community, Prohelp and the Social Enterprise Coalition (now Social Enterprise UK), that she began to really understand both the potential social impact and the pragmatic reality of running a sustainable business. "Between them all, they opened up my eyes to what's expected of you as a business – how it's governed and how it's managed are crucial to its sustainability," Mandy explains. Yet she still remembers her initial lack of understanding and hopes that in the future, social enterprise will be well known as a potential option for anyone thinking of starting an organisation with a social benefit. The combination of understanding the concept of a social enterprise and having the personal drive to make it happen (often based on the key driver's own difficult experiences) could be potent. However, this can only be achieved through education.

"I think it's about educating people at a younger age, what the objectives of social enterprise are. This includes understanding that the sustainability comes from a business ethic. If you did everything just because of the social outcomes, you'd not be sustainable," offers Mandy. She thinks that there is a serious lack of information about social enterprises in business education at school, which, if reversed could have a positive impact on the future of the sector: "If social enterprise was included in learning business at school you'd get more social enterprises." But as Mandy has seen, the absence of social enterprise learning doesn't just stop at school. Adrenaline Alley supports some of its own employees through NVQs in business and management and finds that the programmes do not help them to understand social enterprise. So for those working with her, she asks them to do a presentation on the nature of the business and what that entails: first because she thinks it is a vital part of their business education, but also because she needs to know if people understand the type of organisation they are working for. Put simply: "We need to know, are they on our bus?"

Lack of awareness of social enterprise has a serious knock-on effect for Adrenaline Alley: "If people understood more about social enterprise they'd certainly be more willing to fund it – especially the private sector," Mandy suggests. Also, "when people see you are a charity, they expect things for free. But we're not here to do things cheaper or for less." Mandy hopes that education will be improved so that in the future, these misunderstandings will not happen and social enterprise will be commonplace as another of the options available to people setting up new organisations.

The issue of investment is difficult for social enterprises. While their revenue can come from their activities, Mandy suggests that it can be hard for them to raise enough capital to grow, develop and replicate, especially when any surplus is ploughed back into the social mission. "Raising capital has been our biggest necessity," Mandy explains. She wonders, if social enterprises are not better served by capital funding in the future, whether this could be the one issue that blocks social enterprises from expanding enough to enter the mainstream.

"Keeping trying to find capital to invest is my big issue." Unfortunately even if funds are available, the tax implications of accepting a large lump sum to carry out a capital project can be such that the organisation cannot accept them – "Sometimes you have to refuse funding, as you may not be able to balance VAT and cashflow issues. You pay it [tax] month by month and you get it back months later. If you haven't got £20,000 for the tax cashflow, you can't actually use the £100,000."

Fortunately, Mandy says "I've been so lucky, I've not had anything that's stopped me." She puts some of this 'luck' down to building good relationships with the community, the local authority, private businesses and infrastructure agencies from the start. Now she hopes to build new relationships in the same way to replicate the Adrenaline Alley experience across the country. This is to keep the organisation moving forward and to widen the social impact through other sites, as well as deepen it in Corby. She insists that this replication must involve the same commitment to the local community as she had in the development of her existing site: "If you can give the people what they want, they know you've listened."

Her hope is that in the future the Corby site will be "the Wembley of urban sports" linked to and supporting all the smaller sites around the country.

In order for this to happen, Mandy needs people with passion, capital funds and skills to operate flexibly in an ever shifting market. For some social enterprises the current economic difficulties mean making some hard choices. However, she is hopeful because Adrenaline Alley has a loyal following, a history of growth and achievement and an ambitious plan for the future that should help the organisation to move forward without moving away from its core purpose: to help change young people's lives for the better.

About Mandy Young

Mandy was born and bred in Corby, is married to Paul and they have a daughter named Jodie. Mandy along with her son John (who passed away in September 2010, aged 24) founded Adrenaline Alley in 2002. Mandy is a trustee and development director of Adrenaline Alley and has continued to drive the charity forward. She is responsible for developing Adrenaline Alley making it bigger and better for the future.

Mandy has won many awards for her work, including the BBC Enterprise in Sport award. Mandy needs no excuse for a party, she is well known for her 'wicked' nights out and her love of tequila!

About Adrenaline Alley

Adrenaline Alley is a charitable social enterprise based in Corby that provides urban sports and other facilities (such as a photography studio, performance and practice rooms and support services) to young people from Northamptonshire and further afield. Their mission is to provide a safe and secure environment for people to participate in urban activities. They want to be recognised as a leading provider of urban sports in the UK.

In late 2001, Mandy Young was horrified to learn that her son John had been the target of local bullies. John had struggled through his childhood due to an undiagnosed brain tumour, which resulted in major surgery, radiotherapy and chemotherapy. At 13 years old, he made friends with a group of local skateboarders and he no longer felt the need to explain himself, or worry about his appearance or feelings. However, one night John was attacked viciously by those who knew of his health issues but disregarded them. Mandy and her family were devastated, but were determined to turn the experience into a positive one. After talking with John and his friends they attended a public consultation meeting. It quickly became apparent the intimidation and lack of facilities were a major barrier for young people participating in extreme sports, and that it was not just an estate problem but a national one. With that, Corby Wheels Project was established late in 2002. Support from Rockingham Motor Speedway and Corby Borough Council allowed the project to develop and in July 2003, they opened their gates and hosted 13,000 visitors in 20 months, to become one of the biggest outdoor parks in the UK. Further development and investment by Social Enterprise East Midlands (SEEM) Aimhigher, The Big Lottery People's Millions, WREN and Wooden Spoon enabled the development of an indoor park. In July 2006, Adrenaline Alley opened one of the biggest ramp parks in the UK. Since the opening of the indoor facility, they've hosted over 450,000 visitors and now advertise themselves as the biggest, safest and best urban sports park in the UK, complete with a great atmosphere and welcoming attitude. Their ultimate goal is to improve the lives of young people in Corby and Northamptonshire, giving them a facility over which they have ownership and can be proud of. Their long-term vision is to replicate nationwide and help other communities to develop feeder facilities that will help to ensure that projects such as Adrenaline Alley are safe, secure and sustainable long term in other communities.

MALCOLM HAYDAY
Social enterprise: it's not enough

'Social enterprises could lead the way into an alternative economy that values quality of life above short-term profit-making and that unleashes the power of local communities. In order for this change to come about, politicians, business advisers and, especially, investors are going to have to change their whole approach.'

This is an unexpected response from a banker, but Malcolm Hayday is not your average banker. He started his career in the commercial banking sector before becoming one of the great social finance innovators in the UK. As the founding chief executive of Charity Bank he managed one of the country's biggest social loan funds for 17 years. Malcolm talked extensively about what practical support social enterprises need, before sharing some more radical thoughts about the place of social enterprise in the wider economy.

"The key issue for us was helping people move from having an idea into setting up an organisation. They need to understand that they must make money to sustain their vision." As an investor in social enterprises, Malcolm has a clear view about what support social enterprises need to develop and achieve sustainability. "What they must have is business advice, not advice on how to operate as an NGO. Some of this support must come from other social enterprises but business advisers must be different from the mainstream." Social enterprises need support from experienced and specialist advisers, the traditional business advice for Small and Medium Enterprises (SMEs) is not enough. "The social enterprises that approached Charity Bank generally needed help with marketing, bidding for contracts, planning (so they could identify what they wanted to achieve) and knowing how to measure their impact. It's not a one size fits all approach, but the government doesn't get this."Malcolm recognises that growing a business to scale is fraught with complexities and difficulties. "Currently there isn't enough space for social enterprise managers to take a step back and think about what they want to do and how they want to do it. The external barriers they face are the political and financial orthodoxies that pay lip service to supporting social enterprises".

Our conversation then moved into the relationship between social enterprise and how we want the wider economy to be shaped. "I was at a conference in America recently," he told me, "and there they talk about 'impact organisations', which can include absolutely everything. I decided to provoke everyone and asked if the Mafia is a social enterprise? It could be defined as a mutual organisation that supports its own members and reinvests its profits to share among its members."Malcolm defines social enterprises as having a social purpose that is delivered through trading and that is embedded in the organisation; a democratic structure; and strong roots in a community. "It's important that social enterprises share rewards equitably throughout the business, for example by having narrow pay differentials and rewards paid to all staff not just those in charge."

This is necessary because Malcolm asks some big questions about how society will be shaped. "In 20 years' time we need to have made clear our assumptions about who delivers our services. We could have no public sector left delivering services, just the private sector and social enterprises. Government's only job could be to commission the services. So a bigger issue is how we want our society to operate, what services should be provided by the market place and what do we think should be provided for the benefit of society and help to create a better quality of life?

"I've changed my views on this. I now believe that the economic system is broken and we need to rethink our model of the firm. Social enterprises should be an alternative model of doing business within an alternative system, not a sub-set of the mainstream used to deliver cheap public services. We won't get this unless there is another financial disaster but we should be debating now, what we want delivered and by whom? There are certain things we need to have if we are to live above a subsistence level, such as care for the elderly, transport, a postal service; these things are outside the profit maximisation model. Chocolate bars can be provided by the market but we need a whole alternative system including banks, insurance and pensions that can work with this alternative system because they are part of it."

Malcolm feels that social enterprises are in danger of being "seduced by the men in suits, who are prepared to invest but 'only if you do things our way'. Social enterprises should be prepared to say, 'No, we want to do it this way.' Investors should meet social enterprises at their level, not make them jump through hoops to meet the financiers where they are.

We need a vibrant policy environment so that we can kick around new ideas and peer group reviews of what is working. At the moment we have a pothole economy where we are just filling the gaps, but the long-term costs are phenomenal. We need to think about the kind of society we want for our kids, this should be openly discussed but it isn't."

However, Malcolm warns that social enterprises should also avoid being attached to specific political agendas. "Politicians have an inability to think at grassroots levels."

He concludes, "Social enterprises are entrepreneurial, fleet of foot and innovative. What they do is too important to be left to the open market."

About Malcolm Hayday

Malcolm Hayday's story is in three broadly equal parts. The first third, formal education, resulted in a BA in economics at Exeter University. This was followed by a conventional second third in the world of mainstream finance although in the lesser known parts of consortium banking, petrodollars, trade and Islamic finance, mezzanine and small business funding. Towards the end of this period he began to see that finance could be a very powerful tool for the common good, not just for private gain. For the last 20 years he has immersed himself in the worlds of social finance, innovation and enterprise. He researched, piloted and launched the world's only modern day registered general charity and regulated bank, The Charity Bank, as well as being active in international social banking networks, erstwhile chair of the Big Issue Foundation and contributor to numerous working parties and advisory groups. He stepped down from Charity Bank in 2012 and is now general manager of the Institute of Social Banking and member of the working group for a Scottish community bank. He is also a trustee of Scope and of the Hebridean Whale and Dolphin Trust, when he is not cultivating citrus trees in Andalucia.

STEVE WYLER

Public spending should be 'local by default'

'It's not always a straightforward journey...'

"It's not unrealistic to think that in 20 years' time social enterprise will be much more firmly on the agenda. It could be one of the three big alternatives: public, private, social enterprise," Steve Wyler suggests. While this optimism is grounded in the experience of seeing rapid growth in the sector over the past ten years, he is not claiming that the widespread adoption of the social enterprise model will be easy. For Steve, the key to success will be that each social enterprise is developed in a bespoke way that fits with where and why it is being formed. This means that "it's not always a straightforward journey" and indeed, as businesses, some organisations will fall by the wayside. Yet, this potentially risky and uncharted path is worth following because "where they do succeed financially, they can do more".

Steve adopts a pragmatic definition of social enterprises as businesses trading for a social purpose, but acknowledges the difference within this definition between organisations with social means and social ends: "At the moment it is important to make a distinction between organisations dedicated to doing good in the way they operate and those with an underlying social purpose." He pushes back against what he sees as the "unhelpful" move to replace social enterprise with the term social business to mean any business (even private or public limited companies) that carry out some social function, even if they still return all profit to shareholders. He suggests that their actions "may be laudable, but they are not social enterprises".

As chief executive of Locality (and before that the Development Trusts Association), Steve has long-standing experience with a particular type of social enterprise based in the heart of communities. These community enterprises "have a very strong sense of place, are community-led and operate particularly in deprived areas". These organisations need the right kind of support – what he describes as a "critical friend relationship" – to develop trading options and make sure the business part of the organisation will be sustainable enough to support or carry out the social mission. Steve suggests that "there is by and large a resilience in this way of working" that means community enterprises can still flourish at times of austerity.

Steve's key hope for the future is that there will be "a greater recognition that certain things require a human scale approach". However, he is not suggesting that all social or community enterprises should be small: "I don't necessarily mean organisations that are tiny. Some that are tiny are still awful at human relationships. I mean organisations working with people where they don't standardise [their approach to providing support]. As organisations get larger, it becomes exponentially more difficult…as you become more removed institutionally from people's lives."

Steve thinks that those facing disadvantage would receive better services if there was a move away from standardisation and he suggests that this will be possible if public service commissioning moves to a "local by default" model. This would mean that instead of the public service commissioners putting out one large-scale contract that could only reasonably be filled by a massive, private company, the contracts would be smaller and based more carefully on local need and available local support. "If a greater proportion of spending could be localised, it would reinvigorate the economy, but also provide the opportunity for a more human scale response," Steve believes. This would mean social and community enterprises could contribute to public services, but not replace them: "It's not necessarily either/or. I don't think social enterprise should replace the private or public sectors, but there is some rebalancing to do."

One of the key features of a 'local by default' model is finding ways to make sure that the leadership and ownership of social enterprises truly is local. Steve dismisses any idea that organisations being governed by people from local communities would mean a reduced quality of service: "We're passionate about local people leading. Some of our most successful social enterprises have large boards of people from some of the most disadvantaged estates in the UK. They may not have formal qualifications, but they are capable of a role in top quality social enterprises." This does not mean avoiding using professional help such as lawyers, accountants, architects and others, it just means acknowledging the potential of local people to act and be accountable for those actions.

Steve would be the first to admit that 'local by default' doesn't work for everything: "It would be difficult to see big ticket defence procurement local," but he suggests that, for instance, more community share ownership of successful projects within each area would "democratise ownership" and therefore have a wide-reaching effect of changing who actually gets to own resources in this country.

All of this is part of what Steve sees as the ongoing project of "igniting the impulse to act" within local communities. Some may act to challenge and campaign against current injustices, others may act to create solutions or alternatives. This is where Steve sees social and community enterprises as key in the future. "I think that our fundamental belief is that people, even in adverse circumstances are capable, given half a chance, of adding value. I think that social enterprises at their best create more opportunity for giving people that half a chance."

About Steve Wyler OBE

Steve is the chief executive of Locality, which is growing a nationwide movement of capable community organisations, ambitious for change. Locality was formed in 2011 through the merger of Bassac and the Development Trusts Association, where Steve was director from 2000.

Over the previous 15 years Steve worked for voluntary and community agencies and independent grant-makers. For example in the 1990s, working with homeless agencies, he ran Homeless Network, co-ordinated the Rough Sleepers Initiative in London, and set up Off the Streets and into Work.

Steve has been a member of various government advisory groups on social enterprise, community organisations and the third sector (Cabinet Office, Department for Communities and Local Government, Ministry of Justice). Steve helped to set up the Adventure Capital Fund, and was a Board member until 2011. Steve is currently vice-chair of the Social Enterprise Coalition, and a board member of Thames Reach. He was awarded an OBE in the 2011 New Year Honours List.

About Locality

Locality is the leading nationwide network of community enterprises, development trusts, settlements and social action centres. Locality's membership has expertise in community asset ownership, community enterprise, collaborative working, community voice and advocacy.

Locality assists people to work together to create and capture local wealth for the benefit of communities – giving hands-on support and promoting peer-to-peer exchange.

Locality is running the Community Rights support service with resources, inspiration and advice on using the new Rights including neighbourhood planning, and is leading the Community Organisers programme mobilising people across England. It is also the UK expert on asset transfer, bringing land and building into community hands through the Asset Transfer Unit.

Locality was created through the merger of the Development Trusts Association and Bassac and commenced formal operation in April 2011.

GUY TURNBULL

Almost mainstream, but still very fragile

'All the co-operators I've loved have wanted to change the world and make it a better place.'

Dr Guy Turnbull, managing director of CASA (Care and Share Associates) points out that although a lot has changed in the last 20 years, you still don't go to a bank to start a business and have someone suggest that you become a social enterprise or a co-op. He thinks that if a conventional business fails it is recognised that it can be down to the lack of a market or any number of business problems, but if a social enterprise fails it is often said that it is *because* it is a social enterprise. "I feel there's a huge bank of men in suits waiting for ethical business to fail because we're trying to prove that there is another way of doing business and a fairer way of sharing profits."

Guy has worked in the social enterprise sector for over 20 years, in local government, as a consultant and is also currently vice chair of ICOF, a specialist co-operative loan fund. His role changed as he says, "I got fed up with lobbying from the outside so I decided to make it happen." What he has chosen to make happen is the replication of the award-winning home care co-operative, Sunderland Home Care Associates. His vision for the future of social enterprises is closely linked to the practical steps he is taking to develop CASA. It was set up as a social franchise organisation, helping to replicate SHCA through setting up local, democratic care businesses but with economies of scale such as shared back room services provided by CASA. Guy's vision is that CASA becomes a large national provider, delivering domiciliary care throughout the UK.

He says there are tensions as they have to decide, "Do we go for growth or consolidate to benefit the current members?" At CASA they concluded that one of the main principles of co-operation is to educate others about the model. "We have a duty and an obligation not just to sit comfortably with our own mutual but to export it so that others can benefit."

Guy says that over the years he's spent working with social enterprises he has changed his mind about the central focus of the businesses. "What I've learned is the importance of people. When I started I thought it was all about legal structures but now I think it's vital to have the right people to make things happen. In co-operatives you have a more satisfactory working life and have a better understanding of how businesses work and of your part in the organisation."

He concedes that sometimes it is difficult to get across to people that mutual benefits mean that someone winning doesn't have to be at the cost of someone else losing. "In the right kind of business, people trust each other. They share the benefits and recognise where others need specific benefits." He's developing a programme for people working in the CASA growth initiative to help them engage with the business.

"Although we're owned by the workers they don't always act like it. As we get bigger we have to create economies of scale aligned to proper engagement of the staff. It's more than paying a dividend – individual decisions matter and you have to make the process accessible to everyone so that they understand the role they have to play."

Guy's passion for creating these opportunities is clear as he continues, "I've always believed in mutuality and tried to live my own life according to those principles. It's why I love what I do so much."

However, he and his colleagues at CASA have had to revise their plans to replicate the SHCA. "We asked ourselves, 'Can these individuals do this? Do they have the values, the principles and the entrepreneurial drive?' When I started doing co-operative development in 1991, I thought that anyone could run a business, now I'm not convinced about it. I believe there are loads of Margaret Elliotts [director of Care Services of SHCA who we also interviewed for the book] out there, but we're not good at finding them. As a sector we're meant to be about equality of opportunity. Private capital dismisses individuals without giving them a chance, but we can be too trusting. If we're going to grow we have to spend more resources looking for those kinds of people."

Initially the plan for CASA was to franchise lots of smaller, local organisations. "We couldn't understand why no other people had set up care co-ops in the same way". They wanted to retain the integrity of the model, "rewarding front-line staff doing difficult work, recruiting from excluded and disadvantaged communities and redistributing money – local people looking after local people". Recently though they have taken the decision to merge the franchised organisations into one big employee-owned company. It will provide over 13,000 hours of home care a week, employ 500 carers and have an annual turnover of £8 million. "One reason for doing this," Guy tells me, "is that we need them to be managed well."

Guy thinks that sectors such as care are ripe for social enterprise development. "There are some bits of the economy where social enterprises fit neatly." He does however have some worries. "There are differences between the public, private and social enterprise sectors. Although we provide services for the public sector we don't have a statutory obligation. And what we do is certainly different to the multinationals that give a tiny amount of money back to the community through a corporate social responsibility project."

He continues, "What scares me is the privatisation of the mutual sector. Social enterprises are being created by public sector mutuals as spin-off organisations. We could end up with private capital taking it all back. It's like in the 1980s when loads of employee owned bus companies were set up, but it wasn't long before they were bought out by private businesses. I'm concerned about the mutualisation of public services and I wonder if the aim is to let them fail, then privatise them."

Overall, in his mission to grow social enterprises, Guy is clear about the importance of winning the commercial battle – one of the main reasons he wants to create bigger social enterprises is to be able to compete with the efficiencies of the private sector. "We do need to keep our feet on the ground. You only need two or three organisations to have something go wrong and we're back to the beginning. The vision is to create real exemplars to identify as vehicles that are right for co-op colonisation – we just need the resources to do it. Access to capital is difficult for everyone but it's especially difficult for social enterprises." But for Guy, commercial success will only ever be part of the picture – "All the co-operators I've loved have wanted to change the world and make it a better place."

About Dr Guy Turnbull

Dr Guy Turnbull has been involved in the co-operative and social enterprise sector since 1988, and is now the full-time managing director of Care and Share Associates Limited (CASA).

Previously, he worked across the UK as a social economy consultant, specialising in business planning, training and research and strategic planning. This has included being involved in government policy development, planning and managing multi-million pound projects, helping establish some of the most successful social enterprises around, writing books and much else besides.

Guy is also the elected vice chair and trustee of Co-operative and Community Finance Limited (formerly known as ICOF), a long established and profitable Community Development Finance Initiative.

Guy's main focus of work is as CASA's managing director – driving employee ownership in the health and social care sector.

About Care and Share Associates (CASA)

Care and Share Associates was established in 2004 to provide essential support services to older and disabled people, through developing a franchise network of majority employee owned social care providers. It is based on the award winning Sunderland Home Care Associates model, which has been delivering quality domiciliary support since 1994.

CASA is the UK's leading social enterprise in the social care sector. It currently operates employee owned services across six locations and delivers over 13,000 hours of personal support per week, principally commissioned by the public sector. CASA's mission statement is:

CASA, through its employee owned franchise companies, aims to become the UK's leading employee owned provider of high quality health and social care services. This will be achieved through robust competition with the private sector, and close collaboration with the public sector.

CHRIS DABBS
Social enterprises need to innovate and evolve

'I try to get people to think like eight-year-olds.'

When Chris Dabbs of Unlimited Potential, a ground-breaking Salford based social enterprise, looks to the future of his sector, he hopes that it will be marked by significant innovation and "a permissive environment for the mavericks and outliers – what I have been calling 'positive deviants'". As he sees it, the process of arriving at new solutions to old and intractable problems can easily be stifled if people with authority over new ventures – those commissioning services or leading organisations – don't recognise the value of alternative viewpoints and allow them the opportunity to innovate.

Unlimited Potential has gained increasing recognition by avoiding obvious or accepted ways of addressing social issues, as Chris and his colleagues believe that it is the more fruitful path to making the world a happier and healthier place to live. They have done this through a process of reinventing and renewing the organisation every three years in response to the business environment. They have also changed partners and actively sought out new opportunities.

"I try to get people to think like eight-year-olds. Children get it, adults often don't." Part of this innovative approach is engaging with people in different sectors and fields from those you would necessarily expect to provide inspiration for UK social issues – for instance in manufacturing, design or international development practice, where there are moves towards 'frugal innovation' in developing countries.

Of course, one of the results of crossing boundaries between sectors and fields might be that those boundaries start to mean less. "What would be really good is that the idea of having three sectors [public, private and third] disappears because it has become unnecessary," Chris suggests, enthused that what it means to be an enterprise could be "fundamentally challenged – looking not just to financial accountability but wider impact". While ultimately Chris would like to see the distinction between social enterprises and other organisations disappear, for now, he offers a simple way to assess whether an organisation is or is not a social enterprise: "Fundamentally, the difference is: whatever [social purpose] you're claiming, could you drop it tomorrow?" From his point of view, if the purpose is not built into every aspect of how that organisation operates, inseparably linked to its activities, the organisation is not a social enterprise.

"The **triple bottom line** is built into [Unlimited Potential's] constitution, it's like it's part of our DNA," says Chris. In contrast, he believes that even some of those organisations with legal forms or marketing campaigns that suggest they are social enterprises are not actually part of the sector because they don't share and embed the values that would make them social enterprises. "There are quasi-social enterprises being set up by the public and private sectors. There are also entities of some sort that look like social enterprises – similar to organisations who create something that looks like the genuine Fairtrade mark, but isn't." Chris suggests that there are even private businesses that use social enterprises as "bid candy" – or including social enterprises as attractive potential sub-contractors for public services in bids for work, only to dump or sideline them once the contract has been won. Chris wonders whether these types of initiative, where values are 'for show', not embedded, could harm the social enterprise movement – "There are people who want to take our clothing."

Chris also reminds me, however, that the picture of social innovation is not just about social enterprises and it's also not about *all* social enterprises. First, while there are dangers from other sectors, there are also opportunities and genuine social impact. "For me it is more about focusing on impact, outcomes and values rather than set forms," says Chris, "So some ethical enterprises are better at this stuff than social enterprises." In some places, what might be seen as mainstream businesses are paying attention to their social and ethical responsibilities and going beyond legal requirements, driven by values as well as the desire to profit. Second, "the idea that all social enterprises are angelic is rubbish. Other people in other sectors can be better at [social impact] and it's not a nice neat clearly defined map."

Chris thinks that there is a difference in levels of innovation between the early years of the modern social enterprise sector (from the early 1990s onwards) and the current situation: "16 years ago almost everyone involved [in social enterprises] was genuinely an entrepreneur, breaking new ground," says Chris. As the sector matures, he believes that the social enterprise sector is exhibiting many of the traits of the mainstream business sector: "Most businesses are just copies of other businesses; it's becoming the same in social enterprise, which is fine. It's a bell curve. In terms of innovation most businesses are solid copies, some are behind the times."

"I don't think there's anything necessarily pioneering about being a social enterprise. Social enterprises are just a vehicle for doing stuff." What that 'stuff' is, depends on the organisation's end goal. How it is delivered depends on their values and approach. While Chris notes that a flourishing social enterprise sector in the future could potentially deliver substantially on "more prosaic" social goals like providing adequate housing and appropriate employment, he believes that ultimately social enterprises can be the means to the most important end, promoting "meaningful lives and hope". As a challenge to anyone who might not understand the importance of these more aspirational goals for social enterprise, Chris says, "I know it sounds woolly, but if you don't have hope and love, everything else is irrelevant. There are many people who take these things for granted, but some people can't." Looking to the future, Chris is unsure whether social enterprises will be able to deliver on this agenda, but at their best they could provide a fundamental shift: "If the prevailing environment isn't receptive to [the idea of values guiding business] it won't happen, but if we use social enterprises to shift power in society, that might make a difference."

About Chris Dabbs

Chris has been chief executive of Unlimited Potential since 2005. He has set up, and supported local people to set up, many social enterprises, including through the first community-based social entrepreneurs' programme in the UK, which started in 1999. He is a fellow of the School for Social Entrepreneurs and a fellow of the RSA.

A trained social anthropologist, Chris is an advisor to the Young Foundation, a board member of the Social Value Foundation and chairs the Social Enterprise Council of the Greater Manchester Chamber of Commerce, where he is also a member of the Chamber Council. He is a member of the Manchester Innovation Group, the Health and Well-Being Board for Salford, the Advisory Board of the Centre for Social Business at the University of Salford, and the UpRising Advisory Board for Manchester and Salford. He also advises, or works with, several regional and national bodies on social entrepreneurship and innovation.

About Unlimited Potential

Unlimited Potential is a democratically controlled social enterprise based in Salford that specialises in social innovation for happiness and health. Unlimited Potential operates a range of services, such as Health Trainers, It's A Goal! and Smoke-Free Spaces. At any time, it also runs exploratory social innovation projects to develop new solutions for challenging social issues.

Unlimited Potential was the first organisation in northern England to gain the national Social Enterprise Mark, holds the Investors in People Standard, and is an accredited Living Wage Employer. The Society won Greater Manchester Chamber of Commerce's Innovation Award 2011 and the Innovation Award in the Salford Business Awards 2012. It was shortlisted for the Yunus Social Business Awards 2013, the national Social Enterprise Awards in 2011 and 2013, and the Co-operative Awards 2010, and was highly commended in the National Association of Neighbourhood Management Awards 2009 for its Local Economy Award, for the most enterprising initiative to strengthen the local economy.

SALLY REYNOLDS
Passionate about excellent practice

'The social enterprises that will survive the next 20 years are
the ones that are run well. Full stop.'

Sally Reynolds spent 12 years managing Social Firms UK –
supporting and promoting a particular type of social enterprise called
a social firm that aims to provide real jobs for people facing barriers
to the labour market. She's now heading a large social enterprise:
The Grange. Yet despite this long-term involvement, she is quite
clear that she doesn't "have rose-tinted glasses about the sector" as
a whole. "Social enterprise at its best can change people's lives,"
explains Sally, "but I honestly don't think the social enterprise sector
necessarily holds the magic card. What matters in any organisation
is how it's run."

This means that Sally believes the future of individual social
enterprises will depend more on their internal approach to leadership,
planning, forecasting and knowing their market well, rather than on
any policies or other external initiatives: "The social enterprises that
will survive the next 20 years are the ones that are run well. Full
stop." In the years following the recession of 2009, a number of social
firms closed; Sally wasn't unhappy at seeing some of them and some
of the bigger social enterprises go because she could see that there
were organisations missing the mark on quality and good practice, but
talking themselves up. "I got fed up of people spouting forth about

how brilliant they were, but actually they were glory-seekers and it was all a big show." These contrasted with the excellent social firms and other types of social enterprise, the ones where people would "get on and do the job. You get more respect for that than building it [the social enterprise] up only for people to find out afterwards it's riddled with problems." She was instrumental in setting up the Star Social Firm quality mark because she "wanted that aspiration to excellence in operations across these organisations." One of the factors Sally identified in poor quality social firms was that the people in charge didn't necessarily have the business acumen to operate as a business that truly could provide real goods/services and real jobs at the same time. Sally saw this in the early days of Social Firms UK when statutory organisations (mainly NHS trusts and social services) had false expectations around the social firm model: "Because the agenda was Care in the Community at the time, there were lots of people thinking, 'Oh good, we can just set up a social firm and transfer them [mental health and learning disability service users] all there.'" The problem was, of course, that setting up a business is hard work even for someone who owns and will profit from it. Social enterprises have to be founded on the same hard work, but without the personal profit – and they were sometimes being delivered by people with fixed salaries within a linked public sector organisation. Sally thinks that they might not necessarily have had the same stake in the success of the model as if it had been an independent initiative.

In Sally's view, social firm start-up went one step further than other social enterprises in terms of difficulty: "Out of all the social enterprise models, I'm convinced social firms are the hardest, because they're not aiming to fund some training or support, they're aiming to provide real jobs." Real jobs have to be sustainable. That means treating them as an end in themselves and not just seeing the business as a profit-making adjunct to a larger entity that needs funding. "I don't believe in charities holding onto social firms which they helped create, in order to take a profit. The social firm needs all the profit for itself. If that happens, they are stopping the social firm developing in the future," Sally explains. She saw in some attempts at social firms how a mindset of not taking the rigours of business and the requirements of those disadvantaged employees working within the business seriously enough led to unsatisfactory outcomes for all. Her warning for the future of the sector requires charities and public authorities to learn this lesson: "We saw social enterprises starved of opportunity to provide real jobs when a charity thought it was owed the profit. You have to make sure that larger parent entities don't prevent their own social enterprises from flourishing."

Sally thinks it's very important to look after and encourage future social enterprises, so that the sector doesn't just remain those medium or large organisations that have already set up and managed to survive. "There is no investment in the next generation of social enterprises, just in growing the already fairly big ones. Nobody's thinking about where the new ones will come from," she observes. Also, if social enterprises are expected to provide more and more for society, she wonders if the process of starting them up shouldn't be slightly less hit and miss. Although suitable leaders would need to be found, she suggests that both opportunities and the need for social firms, for example, should be more routinely explored throughout the country to make sure that they could be developed in areas that could benefit: "At the moment we're completely reliant in terms of the luck of the draw on who sets up and runs social firm businesses and where in the country they are. We're dependent on the magic ingredient when someone makes it work."

At The Grange, Sally is already thinking ahead to what the social care market will bring – following her own advice to "keep on top of the market". She sees the organisation's mission as "helping disabled people live more independently and working with them, not to them or for them," which follows a **person–centred approach** where individuals are supported to exercise choice about their lives rather than slotted into services. Sally believes this type of approach, particularly for social enterprises in health and social care, is the way not only to deliver quality, but also to resist pressures from large service commissioners to restrict the type of services to those that only serve the needs of the commissioning budget, rather than the service user: "If the social enterprise delivers quality and puts people at the heart of all its decisions you can stand up against the big boys who aren't necessarily being ethical because they're under financial pressure."

In the future "no organisation should automatically have the 'right to survive' because of the model they are," according to Sally. However, she predicts that – social enterprise or otherwise – organisations with a focus on quality and on people will be the ones that flourish.

About Sally Reynolds OBE

Sally lives and breathes social enterprise and has a background In all three sectors: private, public and third. She helped develop export sales at Duracell, before taking a European-funded role at East Surrey Priority Care NHS Trust. For several years she ran EU-funded projects from the Trust in areas such as supported employment and accessible tourism. She created priority enterprises within the Trust and led in the setting up of Surrey Supported Employment. In 1999 she and a colleague founded Social Firms UK that proceeded to help grow the number of businesses in the social firm sector from just five in 1996 to more than 180 in 2011. She took over as CEO in 2004 and ran the organisation until December 2011.

Sally is passionate about the power of business to change lives and the need for job creation strategies for people who are at a severe disadvantage in the labour market. She was a founding member of Social Enterprise UK and was on its board for several years; she has externalised three social firms from public authorities and was the founding chair of two of them; she is an experienced board director with a significant record of public speaking, lobbying activity, fundraising and business development.

Having left Social Firms UK at the end of 2011 for family reasons, Sally stayed rooted in social enterprise, carrying out work for charities, local authorities and government. She became chief executive of The Grange Centre for People With Disabilities in Bookham (Surrey) in September 2013. She was awarded an OBE in 2012 for services to equality in the labour market.

About the Grange

The Grange is a well-established charity, housing association and social enterprise based in Bookham, Surrey. It provides high quality residential care, Supported Living services, day skills and activities and accommodation for approximately 120 people with learning disabilities. With 110 staff and 117 volunteers, it is well known in the local community and has a 13-acre site where many of its services are based, with others in Bookham, Dorking and Epsom. It is 75 years old and has an annual turnover of approximately £3 million.

Change for people in the UK

If social enterprises do become more prominent in the future, our interviewees suggest that they could provide significant changes for consumers and public service users.

Peter Holbrook thinks that social enterprises can help recalibrate the economy.

Credit unions offer credible alternatives to the big banks in a climate of well-reasoned suspicion of large financial institutions, explains Sally Chicken.

Keith Smith wonders if the general public will take up the challenge of using their spending power in ways that benefit both them and the community.

Michele Rigby hopes that just as consumers have started to embrace environmental messages, they will realise their power to help businesses change lives.

'Why wouldn't you do this?' is the question Tim Smit wants everyone to ask when they hear about social enterprise approaches.

PETER HOLBROOK
Social enterprises can recalibrate the economy

'We've achieved a huge amount in a short space of time and
we need to recognise our achievements.'

Peter Holbrook, the chief executive of Social Enterprise UK does
not need much prompting to share his vision of the future. It is a
future where "social enterprises are a more prominent and visible
part of the UK and global economy, the numbers will increase, the
scale of operations will increase and there will be increased consumer
awareness as people choose to buy from social enterprises". He has
thought about this extensively in his dealings with a wide spectrum
of social enterprises and with policy makers in government and
elsewhere. His vision expands to the point where, "social enterprises
influence how mainstream business operates, to recalibrate the
economy".

Peter describes the current business environment as "mad –
businesses trade and pay taxes to governments to use the money to
solve the problems that sometimes business has created. It's better to
reward businesses that do good things, which means that there will be
less demand on public funds". In order to bring about this change,
Peter thinks that businesses need to operate for all stakeholders, not
just the owners. "It will create a more efficient and fair economy,
which is more resilient, more distributive and more equal." The result
will be that "we can build a society and economy that meets the needs
of 99 per cent of the population not the 1 per cent. Some people
have given up hope and think 'there's nothing we can do about it'."

The cause of this is the lack of trust in business that Peter says has been growing for ten years. "It's partly driven by the recession and the financial crisis, but it's also items on the news about corruption, fraud, bonuses and a sense that business is driven by self-interest." Peter thinks that what will change this view is a more plural and mixed approach to ownership that represents a wide range of stakeholders. This will include individuals, communities, beneficiaries and owners from the public and private sectors and from civil society. He describes this as 'social ownership' and lists some of the stakeholders that could have a role, including pension funds, the Church of England (reflecting the Archbishop of Canterbury's aspirations for credit unions to challenge doorstep lenders in the market place), service users, social investors and private businesses.

The key to raising the profile of social enterprises will be honesty in reporting on performance, against financial, social and environmental measures, leading to greater accountability. This will be important as it will be harder to categorise the many different types of businesses that will develop.

Peter thinks that changes in technology will have an increasingly important part to play. Businesses all over the world will be scrutinised by investigative journalists in the traditional media and citizen journalists using social media. "When someone in a sweatshop in Bangladesh tweets about their working conditions they have immediate access to consumers in the West. They don't need weeks and big budget news programmes to expose stories. People can make their own decisions over who can be trusted."

Although Peter recognises that some people "are jumping on the bandwagon and trying to claim that what they do is social enterprise and that legal definitions are irrelevant", he does believe that the private sector is an important part of the mix and sees a time when "many people in the [social enterprise] sector can draw on their experience of their industry to show that their organisation is committed to operating in a way that balances the interests of the business, society and the planet".

One barrier to development that worries Peter is the lack of the right kind of finance to invest in the growth of social enterprises. He gives one famous example: "Gordon Roddick told me that when they wanted to grow the Body Shop, they needed finance and had to go to the market. They'd set up as a private business because back then, they had no other options. In hindsight he said it would have been better to have gone for social finance if it had been available."

Peter thinks that things are changing, but that change must happen in the right places, "we need to make sure that it's not social enterprises bending to fit in with the finance community. It's not social enterprises that need to evolve and adapt, it's the finance organisations." But this, too, will change as there is more scrutiny by consumers. "There is greater consumer awareness of spending and investment decisions. People need to ask, what happens to your savings and investments? They will make informed decisions about what they buy, where they work and where they save. We already have trusted models such as Fair Trade, this needs to expand into guides to where we work (if we have the choice) and where to invest."

Early in our conversation, Peter gave me his definition of social enterprise off pat, as a man who has been asked the question many times. "Social enterprises are businesses that trade for primary and permanent social or environmental purpose." But he concludes our discussion by reminding me that, "Despite all the introspection in the sector about definitions and all that stuff, we've achieved a huge amount in a short space of time and we need to recognise our achievements." He summarises that this is about a form of business where we have "a notion of doing well and doing good".

About Peter Holbrook

Peter Holbrook is CEO of Social Enterprise UK – the national body for social enterprise. Prior to taking on this role Peter was CEO of Sunlight Development Trust. During his years at Sunlight Peter was responsible for the regeneration, through social enterprise, of some of the UK's most deprived communities. He developed 'project sunlight', based in Gillingham, Kent, from its inception to become an award-winning 'community anchor'. In 2007, Peter was appointed to be one of the UK's Social Enterprise Ambassadors – a scheme supported by the Cabinet Office and coordinated by Social Enterprise UK. In this role he advocated for social enterprise through lobbying politicians, speaking at events and representing the sector in the media.

In 2010, Peter was appointed as a member of the Cabinet Office's Mutuals Taskforce and trustee of the Big Society Trust (overseeing delivery of Big

Society Capital). In 2012, he was appointed a member of the EU Social Business Initiative Expert Group and took up the role of chair of the Social Enterprise World Forum.

About Social Enterprise UK

Social Enterprise UK is the national body for social enterprise. Its members are social enterprises and other types of organisations that support or have an interest in social enterprises. Social Enterprise UK lobbies and campaigns to raise the profile and understanding of social enterprise, regularly carries out research into the state of the social enterprise sector in the UK and hosts events and activities that bring people involved in social enterprise together.

Social Enterprise UK was previously known as the Social Enterprise Coalition and was initially established in 2002 to co-ordinate and present a united voice for the variety of existing organisations working with and in the social enterprise sector.

SALLY CHICKEN
How the law can make or break social enterprises

'I'm not asking for any great advantage, I just want to compete fairly.'

Everywhere Sally Chicken has lived, she has been involved in a **credit union**. She spoke to me in her capacity as a director of the Ipswich and Suffolk Credit Union, which she was involved in setting up and which opened its doors in 2002. Over the years she has seen how each change in legislation has helped or hindered the sector's growth as an alternative to the high street banks. This insight runs through and informs her vision of the future – a future where credit unions are allowed by law to come into the mainstream to compete on fair terms with the big banks.

Sally suggests that "20 years ago a credit union was little more than a safe savings account" and could offer very few other services. "It was difficult to do anything slightly different," Sally remembers, "so, we started lobbying hard to get the law changed." In 2002, the Financial Services Authority (FSA) took over regulation of credit unions from the Registry of Friendly Societies and this meant that they were covered by the financial services compensation scheme – a central fund held by the FSA to compensate savers if UK banks, building societies and credit unions go bust. This change in legislation and consequent regulation had an instant effect on the credit union offer: "It immediately made us more legitimate – previously people weren't saving much money with us" because it would not have been protected, Sally explains.

"When the FSA started looking at us, I said, 'This is a good thing,' as they looked at us from a financial services point of view," says Sally. This meant creating a more open market for financial services and allowing credit unions to cater more to the needs of their members. Since that point, and following more recent legislation in 2012, credit unions have been able to offer a wider range of services to a wider range of members. Sally describes how their credit union has embraced the latest available technology and new offers like the ISCU pay-as-you-go debit card have "been a huge leap forward and have helped us to extend our community banking".

So, in this way, changes in legislation and regulation have helped credit unions to grow and change for the good of the community. However, Sally also notes that certain aspects of the 2012 legislation – on which big banks were consulted – still restrict credit unions in a number of ways: "Legislation is sometimes deliberately framed – or so it seems – to create barriers that stop us growing." Sally gives examples: "For instance, we're limited in that up to 25 per cent of our customers can be businesses. At some point that will hold us back. It isn't at the moment but it will. So that's not an open, free market."

When I ask Sally what could justify restricting the potential of credit unions, she speculates whether legislation has been influenced by a paternalistic attitude towards people who are trying to work co-operatively, some of them on a voluntary basis, or to put it simply, an attitude of: "You don't know what you're doing." She reminds me that the potential size of credit unions is not limited by their nature, just by legislation: "In other countries [credit unions] are an alternative to the mainstream. In America and Australia we are as big as the banks." So Sally's future vision involves lobbying successfully for credit unions to enter the market squarely alongside the big banks: "I'm not asking for any great advantage, I just want to compete fairly."

Sally's previous point about credit unions being limited to 25 per cent business customers by law also has its own significance for the social enterprise sector, as well as being illustrative of the restrictions credit unions work under. As a number of social enterprise practitioners have also stated, Sally would like to buy from social enterprises. "Everything we spend, I look and say 'Could we get that from a social enterprise?'" says Sally, but finds the number and range of social enterprises selling business services is limited. "Many social enterprises see their service as providing to the public, not business to business," suggests Sally, "but they could be doing both." If social enterprises could source financial services from other social enterprises – what could the potential be for changing the whole investment and funding environment? Given the vexed issue of suitable investment in the social enterprise sector, the potential could be great. Additionally, Sally thinks more extensive business to business buying for social enterprises in general "could help [social enterprise] become more mainstream".In the future, Sally would like to see the registration of social enterprise status on Companies House records. While there have been various online databases and registers for social enterprise these have usually been created as part of an initiative around a particular type, area or sector and represent just part of the sector at a snapshot in time. "Anyone can look anything up on Companies House, it's an easy thing you can do and that doesn't happen with other registers," Sally explains, hoping for a clear way to identify any businesses that are mainly reinvesting profits for the good of the community or the sustainability of the social enterprise. Yet this change would also require regulatory reform and government definition of qualifying criteria. As a whole, Sally's future vision suggests that the law can make or break social enterprises' and, specifically credit unions' chances of entering the mainstream. She sums up: "You've *got* to have the underpinning legislation in place."

About Sally Chicken

Sally Chicken, MSc, enjoys living in the Suffolk countryside. She has helped start five credit unions in the last 20 years and is currently a volunteer director at two credit unions: Ipswich and Suffolk Credit Union and Rainbow Saver Anglia Credit Union. Recent projects include merger activity with neighbouring credit unions, participation in the national Credit Union Expansion Plan (CUEP) and the opening of a new Rainbow Saver branch in Peterborough, which resulted in more than 700 new members in the first six months of trading.

Her paid work is as an elected director of the East of England Retail Co-operative Society, one of the largest independent retail co-ops in the UK. Sally is particularly proud of the Society's commitment to locally sourced food production.

Sally studied for a part-time MSc at the University of Glamorgan while starting Cardiff Credit Union, and the subject of her dissertation was 'A workplace credit union: a case study analysis of Paysaver'.

KEITH SMITH
Keep true and keep going

'Turning begging on its head'

"I see social enterprises as a blend of communism and capitalism and trying to knock the edges off both," says Keith Smith, director of the Ferry Project, a social enterprise that provides accommodation and personal development opportunities for people facing homelessness. "I don't accept the idea that people can own social enterprises, but that they're more like charities: regulated by the crown, managed by the people for the good of all." For Keith, this idea makes the managers and directors of social enterprises stewards for the social purpose that the organisation is trying to create and differentiates social enterprises from other businesses which create social outcomes, but also distribute profits in some way: "You're still pulling money out of the community to give it to individuals."

Instead, Keith acts according to the principle of "turning begging on its head". This approach has been particularly informed by his experience of developing a small accommodation organisation for homeless people into a large social enterprise with multiple income streams: "Homeless people are thought of by many as beggars, so if we as an organisation just replace the homeless person by asking for money, this won't change." Keith is sensitive to the idea that not every socially desirable activity currently funded charitably can directly earn income, but he does wonder whether more organisations might not be able to make a surplus through one activity to support another socially worthwhile activity elsewhere and in doing so, adopt this principle. The Ferry Project example of providing a shop, café and function room as well as different types of accommodation follows this model.

While these activities do indeed provide training opportunities for people housed by the Project, Keith thinks that running a purely business activity to provide a useful surplus for the organisation is within the spirit of social enterprise: "If I run a business that just gives people some pleasure and do that the best I can, then I know the surplus will be used to do good things. I don't have a problem with that." He thinks that if social enterprises concentrate on providing surpluses in the future by developing robust business models and planning for growth, then they will be able to do more and more good. He doesn't see increasing in scale as a problem for social enterprises and cites existing large business operations where the surplus is being used for the benefit of communities: "Think of Norway, a place where there is hydro-electric power and the profits are given to local government."

Keith sees great potential for surplus-generating activities to benefit communities rather than individuals: "Once the snowball gets going there's a real opportunity." But he is also sanguine about the time it might take this idea to filter into general practice. "I think 20 years into the future is too small a timescale. Growing up and maturing takes hundreds of years," suggests Keith. He also believes that there will still be private, public and social enterprise organisations to provide balance in society, but with more blurring around the edges and shifts in income source from taxation to social enterprise purchases. In the future, he suspects a big difference might be scale: "You might have a few social enterprises going for larger [public service] contracts, because they have become mature enough to do that."

According to Keith, it's not just a question of social enterprises maturing – it's also a matter of what people in general will accept: "Let's be real and accept each of us is selfish to one extent or another, so the question is, to what extent can we, as a whole society, cope with the idea that doing good to someone else will cost a little." For Keith, this is the key issue for the future of social enterprises. At their best, he suggests that they can act to equalise the use of wealth for well-being across society, because those who can buy things from social enterprises do and those who need support from them can then have it – in the same way as taxation for the welfare state was conceived. However, he sees this idea as "a challenge" to many in Britain and wonders if social enterprise became more widespread, whether "some people who want to be more affluent than others will reject the model because they want to benefit [from businesses] personally."

Finally, but importantly, Keith sees the inherent equalising role of social enterprises as playing a key part in a much needed shift in social initiatives towards prevention rather than response to existing issues. "It's very difficult to pursue a preventative agenda, because it's a massive barrier in people's minds to fund against what might not happen. If you are successful, you stop it! It's very difficult but very real and you need people who understand that." Using social enterprise could potentially bypass some of these issues because of its indirect form of funding – the available surplus can be used on visionary preventative projects. Keith hopes that the future of the Ferry Project will include activities to foster involvement and interaction in the community, provide spaces to do this and provide opportunities for those who are marginalised – all to try to tackle problems before they start, rather than once things have gone too far.Keith thinks that it is only natural that trying to introduce these ideas of self-sufficiency, acceptance and prevention into common practice will take time and it will take perseverance. "An example to draw on is the great Victorian philanthropists – they did so much but then got distracted into capitalism," Keith suggests, adding "so what we need to do is keep true. And keep going!"

About Keith Smith

Keith Smith is married with five grown-up children and has lived in Wisbech for the last 30 years. Keith has a degree from University of Reading in chemistry and food science and was a secondary school chemistry teacher and pastoral deputy head for 16 years. He is also a trained counsellor and practised for three years.

Keith left teaching due to damaging the muscles around his vocal chords that resulted in him being unable to speak totally for four months and then taking another two years to learn how to speak again with the help of speech therapists.

Keith started The Ferry Project, in 1998. It is a social enterprise and registered charity providing support and accommodation to homeless people which he now manages as director. In 2010 Keith won Fenland business person of the year and in 2012 was voted Inspirational leader of the year by the Chartered Institute of Housing.

He was a board member for Social Enterprise East of England (four years) and Cambridgeshire Community Reuse and Recycling Network (four years) and chair of governors for Leverington Village Primary School (six years). Keith has no accredited training in business but is personally mentored by Dr Chan Abraham CEO of Luminus Group, of which Ferry Project is a subsidiary company, as a member of his Leadership Academy.

About Ferry Project

Ferry Project is a charity that aims to help homeless single adults, in the Fenland area, by providing both emergency accommodation and longer-term help. It was founded in 1998 by members of Wisbech Churches Together and joined Luminus Group in March 2006. Their aim is to help people move on to their own independent living with a home of their own and a job.

In March 2006, Ferry Project became part of Luminus Group. Ferry Project still has its own board and management but receives a lot of support and help from Luminus, a socially responsible business that is widely recognised for its inspirational approach to providing homes, building communities and highly motivated employees. Luminus has helped by purchasing property for Ferry Project to use and by supplying affordable services to Ferry Project.

They offer short- and long-term accommodation for single people from a range of backgrounds who have various needs. These cover those who have financial problems, people recovering from family breakdown, those recovering from drug and alcohol abuse, young people leaving the care system, the sexually abused, ex-offenders and those with nowhere else to go. Their time with the project can be for one night or up to 18 months. People come into Ferry Project via Octavia View, their beautiful grade 2 listed community hub in the centre of Wisbech. People can stay in the hostel in Octavia View for up to six months before moving on to a shared flat or bedsit. In Octavia View residents receive support 24 hours a day. They learn a variety of skills to help them live more successfully in their own accommodation and they get love and support to help them manage their problems. During the time people are with Ferry Project they are helped to consider their future and the options they have available to them. Ferry Project works with a range of partners to help the residents get back into their own home with a job.

They run an emergency night shelter, and a direct access hostel in Wisbech. When residents are ready for more independent living they progress to a first stage move in accommodation in Mill Close or Friends Court. Finally they move into their own home either with a housing association or a private landlord. Ferry Project helps them to find this accommodation.

MICHELE RIGBY
A cultural shift towards happiness

"Ten years ago I would have said that the future goal of social enterprises should be to be invisible – part of the fabric. I completely disagree with myself now: visibility is key."

Over the course of the last 20 years, Michele Rigby has been a significant part of the social enterprise world, as managing director of social enterprise Recycle-IT!, as CEO of Social Enterprise East of England and, more recently, of Social Firms UK. So when she says she has changed her opinion completely on what the social enterprise movement most needs, you know it's coming from experience. "Maybe in 30 years' time buying from social enterprise will be as much a no-brainer as sorting your rubbish, but for now we need visibility."

"What we have to do is look at where big cultural shifts have happened in the past," Michele explains as we discuss how social enterprises might become part of the mainstream in the future, "and the environmental shift is the key one". As we talk about the environmental movement of 30 years ago, Michele highlights how far thinking on the environment and business has come: "When I started out, if you talked about the environment in the private sector, even in the public sector, you'd be laughed off the platform. Whereas these days you can't do any type of business without an environmental record. It would tarnish your reputation and damage your business."

Could we feasibly reach a point in the future where not deeply embedding social responsibility in your business model could result in the same kind of damage? "We've done it with the environment within 30 years…" Michele suggests, but with caution, acknowledging that the varied messages of social impact across the sector may be harder to convey in a "blanket" way. "As a sector it can be as large as the general public want it. If we as a people want to embrace it, there'll be more social enterprise. If we don't embrace it, there won't be more of it."

As we discuss the ways this cultural shift could be accomplished, Michele suggests that changes are needed both at supply and demand side to make it work. On the part of social enterprises, there's a responsibility to campaign to raise visibility collectively and "be more confident. I think there's still a problem for the sector as a whole that we're still asking permission to exist, in some ways – in ways you wouldn't expect from a private sector business."

If better confidence and visibility was accomplished by the sector, then social enterprise mainstreaming would rely on customers – both from the general public and public sector commissioners – understanding and weighing up the consequences of their purchasing decisions. Michele suggests that all consumers do this already, quite happily, on other grounds: "We're very prepared to pay more as consumers for some products because we understand the R&D [research and design] that went into them…We don't want producers like Apple to charge us too little – we want them there for the future, we're buying for the future too." The key will be fostering that understanding of the long-term benefits of social enterprises (and the importance of investing in the work that has gone into making those benefits) to those who hold the purse strings.

Michele's vision of the future, then, is of a growing period of awareness and visibility for social enterprises to reach a point where combining commercial success and providing a social benefit is not just "tolerated" but "embraced" by consumers. This would also provide practical help to those setting up social enterprises and running social enterprises, because it would mean that they would not have to constantly explain their motivation for suggesting innovative combinations of business and social benefit to those who might provide advice, seed-funding or custom to them. The sector could move beyond working hard to justify themselves, to simply making their offer – a really important step that needs to take place.

And, according to Michele, the social enterprise offer could be a profound one: "Where there's inequality, all people are less happy – even those with more within that society. One of the things with which social enterprises are concerned is equality and fairness. So as a sector we should be promoting on the grounds of happiness." And this happiness does not have to come at the expense of a flourishing capitalist economy – that's one of the myths that needs to be challenged: "The danger is confounding social enterprise with charity – it can be hard to get the message of social impact over alongside the message of commercial success." Getting people to understand the difference between philanthropy and mutuality is key to challenging this myth.

Ultimately, the message can be quite simple: "Happiness, health and money are things everyone thinks they could do with more of." So if while participating in the economy on the same terms as other businesses (producing wealth that stays in the community rather than being distributed to remote shareholders), social enterprises also bring happiness – who wouldn't agree with that argument? The key, then, is getting it out to the world and showing that a different way of doing business has implications for everyone: "Everybody that doesn't have a job and gets a job because there's a **social firm** or a **work integration social enterprise** set up near them – that makes them happy. It makes their family happy and their community happy. So social enterprise is about working and about business, but it's also about equality and happiness. That must surely fit with every possible political persuasion."

About Michele Rigby

Michele Rigby is CEO of Social Firms UK – the national support and membership organisation for the development of the Social Firm and Work Integration Social Enterprise (WISE) sector in the UK. Michele joined Social Firms UK in January 2012. Before that, she was CEO of Social Enterprise East of England (SEEE) from April 2006 to November 2011.From 1995 to 2005, she co-founded and managed Recycle-IT! Ltd, an award-winning social firm with a global market. Through the social firm, work experience, training and paid employment were offered to the long-term unemployed. Recycle-IT's recycling activities involved IT equipment data-wiping and disposal services for major corporates, local authorities and small businesses – all underpinned by a commitment to good environmental working practices.

Michele's experiences at the sharp end of setting up and running an award-winning social firm, and of leading both national and regional social enterprise support bodies informs her views on the needs of social firms and the wider social enterprise sector, and the policy directions that enable and encourage them both to occupy a proper space within the national economy, and to bring new ways of effecting social change.

She has also been a board member of Social Enterprise UK, and a council member since 2009. She served on the DTI Small Business Council, and has been a director of Investors in People UK.

About Social Firms UK

Social Firms UK is the national membership and support organisation for the development of the **social firm** and Work Integration Social Enterprise (WISE) sector in the UK. These are employability-focused social enterprises that believe that everyone has the right to be employed and support those furthest from the labour market.

Social Firms UK carries out lobbying and awareness-raising activities, research and practical initiatives to support employability focused social enterprises across the UK. Examples of these include the business support tool InfoMine, www.socialfirmsinfomine.org.uk, the operation of the only accredited quality scheme in the social enterprise sector (Star), a wide range of online resources for start-up and developing social firms, visits across the sector to share good practice and for educational, training and personal development.

In response to increasing demand from the corporate sector to purchase services and supplies from social enterprises, Social Firms UK offers expertise and management in developing procurement strategies that develop values-led supply chains by managing key relationships, providing opportunities for pro bono support and secondments, and promoting the development of ethical purchasing through the 'Just Buy' campaign online with its accompanying inter-trading website: www.justbuy.org.uk.

SIR TIM SMIT
The 'win–win' approach

'Why wouldn't you do this?'

At the start of our interview, Tim Smit is keen to warn me that he's "quite brutal about" how we should be thinking about social enterprise. He foresees massive potential to transform people's lives through social enterprise approaches, if only the sector could avoid being made "un-robust by hippyness". What Tim wants to see in the future is a strong and clear message reaching beyond those who are already interested in social enterprise and capturing the imagination of bright young men and women who might otherwise go into high-powered professional jobs in large corporations. "Some of the smartest minds in our society are seduced into high end capitalism because we haven't given them a different narrative to follow," he explains, but goes on to warn: "The narrative of social enterprise should not seek to demonise the creation of wealth. For those people with the potential for achieving personal wealth, that should remain." For Tim, the problem is the demonisation of profit and "a whole series of knee jerk reactions to business" that he believes sometimes seem to accompany ideas of generating social good.

The idea of making the social enterprise approach attractive to top professional people through adequate reward is the first of many examples in this interview where Tim's future vision is about promoting 'win–win' situations. Yet, he's clear that each side does not have to be equally balanced in this equation. The idea of finding an "appropriate (that doesn't mean equal)" balance forms one of the pillars of Tim Smit's understanding of what makes a social enterprise. "To me the difference between a social enterprise and a non-social enterprise currently has two parts: first is how the **equity** is distributed. Second is the degree to which there is benefit to the wider community and proportionality of personal reward appropriately balanced to that." Tim prefers not to set thresholds or ratios for the balance but thinks that appreciating whether an organisation is a social enterprise or not is based on a holistic understanding of what it does, what results and who gets the benefit.

He goes on to add a third point to his understanding of social enterprise, but this time it's something he'd like to see define the approach in the future. "A social enterprise, in its memorandum and articles, could feasibly define what it means by profit," Tim suggests. "Profit can't possibly be just about money." Tim's future vision is one where the wider impact of each organisation is considered in the audit process. As an example, he suggests that the return on the level of investment needed to bring about The Eden Project, if judged solely on the organisation's annual turnover, would not seem reasonable. For him, it's the wider understanding of Eden's contribution that proves it's worthwhile: "We've put £1.3 billion back into the [local] economy."

Looking beyond the financial and thinking about what social enterprise activity means for the environment and society is, apparently, gaining ground all over the globe. For instance, in China, Tim has spoken to "a whole bunch of young guns coming through; well-educated, aware their country is being trashed environmentally but they know they can't sustain it". Whereas former communist countries such as Russia ended up with oligarchies as a result of economic restructuring, these new thinkers in China "see social enterprise as part of the antidote to oligarchy" says Tim. He suggests that social enterprise provides the kind of compromise the Chinese economy could accommodate: "It answers the question – how can they take the sexiness of capitalism, but have the honourable position of not just having wealth for a particular stakeholder group?" In such a massive economy, the potential of adopting social enterprise approaches could have far-reaching effects for the way the world does business. Tim suggests that our experience to date means that we, in the UK, could have great influence on this if we continue to develop the idea of social enterprise in the right direction.

With this in mind, Tim offers a radical suggestion of how to ensure social accountability: the government should have a golden share in every business, that allows it to audit the business and identify the contribution it makes to the national interest.

The traditional definition of a golden share is when a government retains a residual share when privatising a company – which allows it limited powers to veto certain major changes to the company, like mergers or takeovers. What Tim is suggesting is that all companies, whoever owns them and whatever their purpose, would have to agree to the government golden share in order to be incorporated – making them more accountable for their impacts.

In the absence of this approach, which would be revolutionary in its effects, Tim's current practice is to focus on getting organisations to understand what they get out of acting more like a social enterprise (again, a win–win), rather than thinking that changes mean extra costs and a reduction in market advantage in comparison to their competitors. It's about, "seducing people gently into different ways of working," according to Tim, and working with individuals who may genuinely want to do things differently as long as they are offered ways to do it that don't damage the organisation. Tim thinks that social media have helped greatly because companies find out what has an impact on their reputation more clearly and more immediately: "It's about setting benchmarks of 'Why wouldn't you do this?'"One way of working out a win–win approach to an activity could involve extensive **stakeholder engagement** with the local community. Tim is a believer in the power of this approach, but only if it's done right. "My experience is that if you have time to inform anyone fully about the decision they will come to the right decision – with Eden, we took the time." He describes the process of allowing local people the opportunity to comment, then going away and changing things as a result of those comments: "They [the local people] were amazed! Most [other organisations] treat engagement as a form of broadcast." The pay-off for Eden was trust and fantastic un-solicited suggestions for how to deal with planning bumps they hit along the way. Even in situations where Eden has consulted and been knocked back by locals over certain activities, Tim still sees the situation as a win–win – just one where the win for Eden is longer-term: "We lost, but the win was in trust. The future win will be in an area where the loss is not so bad for them."

This type of pragmatic understanding of how to balance the aims and needs of different stakeholders suffuses Tim's discussion of social enterprise. He wants to see "the standards of doing great business" applied to social enterprises, but also to make sure that they are constantly challenging and pushing forward more appropriate practices, for example: "A great and professional social enterprise movement needs to challenge the logic of 1980s privatisations. Social enterprises running these businesses would be much better – and I include the trains in that!"

Tim Smit thinks that social enterprise will enter the mainstream "if we are grown up about it". For him this means professionalism, intelligent government and good use of available capital – including allowing big business to have some equity in social enterprises if, pragmatically, it would be the most effective way of helping them achieve their purpose. This all suggests to him that: "any social enterprise should be run by a pragmatist with a heart of gold".

About Sir Tim Smit KBE

Sir Tim Smit KBE is chief executive and co-founder of the award-winning Eden Project near St Austell in Cornwall. Born in Holland in 1954, he read archaeology and anthropology at Durham University before going on to work for ten years in the music industry as composer/producer in both rock music and opera. In 1987 Tim moved to Cornwall, where he and John Nelson together 'discovered' and then restored the Lost Gardens of Heligan. Tim remains a director of the gardens to the present day.

As well as his contribution to the Eden Project, Tim is a trustee, patron and board member of a number of statutory and voluntary bodies both locally and nationally. In January 2011 he was appointed an honorary Knight Commander of the Most Excellent Order of the British Empire (KBE) by Her Majesty the Queen. This appointment was made substantive in June 2012 when he became a British Citizen. He has received honorary doctorates and fellowships from a number of universities. In 2011 Tim was given a special award at the Ernst & Young Entrepreneur of the Year Awards, which recognises the contribution of people who inspire others with their vision, leadership and achievement.

Tim is the author of books about both Heligan and Eden and he has contributed to publications on a wide variety of subjects.

About The Eden Project

Eden began as a dream in 1995 and opened its doors to the public in 2000, since when over 13 million people have come to see what was once a sterile pit turned into a cradle of life containing world-class horticulture and startling architecture.

The Eden Project was built in a 160-year-old exhausted china clay quarry near St Austell, in Cornwall. It was established as one of the Landmark Millennium Projects to mark the year 2000. The initial idea was conceived in the light of Tim Smit's experiences while working on the restoration of the Lost Gardens of Heligan – an experience of the stories that connect plants and people.

The most visible symbols of the Eden project are the massive biomes – large faceted glass structures – where you can find 'the largest jungle in captivity', a waterfall, thousands of tropical and Mediterranean plants and the biggest flower in the world. The visitor attraction also includes gardens, an educational centre, play areas, trails, adventure activities and ample opportunity to eat and drink. It is also a venue for corporate entertaining and private venue hire.

The Eden Project is one of the most prominent and recognised social enterprises in the UK. The Eden Project is a company limited by guarantee and is wholly owned by the Eden Trust, a UK Registered Charity. Running the business in this way means that when people spend money having a good time at the Eden project, it helps the organisation to develop transformational social and environmental projects, provide innovative educational programmes, do valuable research into plants and conservation and run their operations in the greenest possible way.

Eden has contributed over £1 billion into the Cornish economy. The organisation is proud of its success in changing people's perception of the potential for and the application of science, by communicating and interpreting scientific concepts through the use of art, drama and storytelling as well as living up to its mission to take a pivotal role in local regeneration. According to the organisation, all of this success "demonstrates once and for all that sustainability is not about sandals and nut cutlets, it is about good business practice and the citizenship values of the future".

FIVE

A social enterprise movement for the future: an overview

The Voices that comprise the core of this book have offered us the chance to hear from people who run, support, research and create policy around social enterprises. Each piece has revealed what people involved in the social enterprise sector are passionate about, their values and how they believe the actions of their social enterprise will change society and the economy. Many of them bring years of experience to this discussion. As well as looking forward with hope and expectation, they have also been frank in highlighting difficulties and barriers – both for individual organisations and for social enterprises in general. They have informed us of new or emerging ideas and offered their particular solutions to pressing challenges along the way. Yet, even more crucially for the future of social enterprise, their contributions have provided further questions, challenged the status quo and highlighted divergent ways forward for the sector.

In this chapter we reflect on how the knowledge and experience that people have shared with us can assist in thinking about the future of social enterprise development. In the introduction to this book, our stated aim was to help people involved in social enterprises, or interested in them, to be clear about how their own goals, politics and life experience affect how they see social enterprises develop in the future. We hoped that greater clarity on these issues would help people to start up and develop appropriate and successful social enterprises (and, equally importantly, choose not to in particular contexts) and have fruitful debates about what is important in the management, governance and market positioning of those social enterprises.

The following interpretations are offered in this spirit – not of promoting any one specific future route for social enterprise definitions or practices, but instead offering clarity on how the different parts of the jigsaw that is the social enterprise movement may contribute to a variety of different agendas and address a range of problems in society. Each Voice in this book represents a single piece of the jigsaw that we have chosen to piece together around the core concept: 'organisations trading in order to improve the well-being of people in the UK'. Yet, the Voices offer us glimpses of how different social, environmental and political preoccupations could form the centre point of a jigsaw where social enterprise is just one contributing piece. This means that in order to take the sector forward with clarity, everyone involved in the social enterprise movement needs to question their own motives and priorities and answer for themselves the key question: why social enterprise and to what ends? We hope that the discussion below provides impetus for this questioning process.

A movement?

By comparing social enterprise development to that of the women's movement, the environmental movement and the standardisation of financial accounting, our interviewees have been able to point out that these previous campaigns achieved eventual widespread change, but also experienced difficulties and delays along the way. However, thinking of social enterprises as a movement also helps us to focus clearly on the question: what is a social enterprise movement a movement towards? The Voices of those who research social enterprise, such as Fergus Lyon and Roger Spear, and those who have developed new approaches to categorising and measuring them, such as Lucy Findlay and Jeremy Nicholls, have contributed valuable perspectives to the sense of a growing movement and the directions such a movement might take. For instance, at the heart of Jeremy Nicholls' interview is the movement towards *greater business accountability*, with social enterprises potentially playing a role alongside the wider business community in challenging the status quo. In the piece featuring Lucy Findlay, the emphasis is instead on *how profits made by businesses could serve other – more broadly socially beneficial – purposes in the future*, with social enterprises as the vanguard movement. The end goal is subtly different although clearly complementary.

These subtle (and sometimes not so subtle) differences in end goals can be found throughout the Voices section. For some interviewees it is possible to read between the lines and suggest that one of the most important features of their organisations is whether they are *innovating* for social good. Chris Dabbs, for instance stated that he wanted to see "a permissive environment for the mavericks and outliers" – or "positive deviants". These innovators are aiming to benefit society by leading the way for other organisations to follow. For others what was once seen as the 'innovative' combination of business means and social ends in the social enterprise approach simply provides the earned income to fund tried and tested techniques that *support and help* vulnerable people. Keith Smith, for instance is pragmatic about this take on social enterprise: "If I run a business that just gives people some pleasure and do that the best I can, then I know the surplus will be used to do good things. I don't have a problem with that."

For some social enterprises, belief in the participative element is key. There would be no point to what they do if they were not listening to, engaging and therefore *empowering* their membership and the communities in which they operate. Jenny Sims provided an example of the importance of member control to social enterprise. Yet in our interview she also demonstrates the way in which outsiders, rooted in the norms of mainstream business, failed to understand the importance of the values of that particular business. This provides an illustration of how mainstream concepts of 'social good' often overlook goals that relate to redistributing power in society and the solidarity fostered by collective action.

For other social enterprises, the pressing practical, material and psychological concerns of the vulnerable people they aim to help prompt them to seek guidance on how to deliver greater efficiency and effectiveness in the provision of social goods and services. They draw on good practice lessons from successful mainstream businesses. Only by being what June O'Sullivan calls "best in class" can these people see social enterprises *providing a significant scale and quality of social outcomes*.

It is important to note that the different options given above are not in opposition. If the Voices section tells us anything it is actually that within the interviews the same people can at different times espouse different priorities and, for instance, combine a commitment to wider participation in one element of their organisation with a preference for a lean hierarchy in another. They can work with people with different end goals and motivations in mind and therefore construct organisations that represent many different values and concerns at once. Multiplied up throughout the sector, this provides a perfect illustration of how the movement is trying to move in many directions at once and both forging new ground through a combination of methods and values and seemingly pulling against itself in the process. A common response in the past has been for those within the movement and others viewing it from outside, to focus on these differences as oppositional. However, they can equally be seen not as divergent but as multi-stranded and complex. The danger is not in the complexity of the movement but from those who seek easy solutions and to pigeon-hole organisations according to their own assumptions about the nature of social enterprises.

Points of convergence

Fergus Lyon and Jeremy Nicholls, among others, highlighted how the future of social enterprises could either be as a smaller, tightly defined sector of organisations trading for social purpose or a sprawling, loose family of different processes and approaches operating to provide social change. While it is possible to position these two as divergent futures (where not defining social enterprise means it becomes devoid of all meaning and value as a term), it is also possible to see them as two sides of the same coin.

Just as the suffragists and the suffragettes differed in their approaches to lobbying for change, we have seen in the Voices section the varied approaches that even one country (the UK) can offer. It can be argued that it was the combination of the suffragist, suffragette and other women's advocate campaigns that contributed to social change for women, alongside the timely intervention of two world wars giving women the chance to prove their case for equality by taking on new roles and responsibilities (reminding us that external factors are incredibly important unknowns in any future prediction). In the same way it can be argued that different approaches to social enterprise could work towards the same ends if they are clear about when they are and are not pulling in the same direction, and why.

The following discussion explores points of similarity and difference to help reach this understanding.

The interviews you have just read took place four to six years after the global financial crisis of 2008, which resulted in loss of trust in traditional business and finance institutions, and in the context of a UK political climate stressing the need for austerity in public spending. One of the most striking recurring themes we identified during the research process was the extent to which this made our interviewees reflect on whether social enterprise approaches had 'come of age'. Would social enterprises be recognised as offering credible alternatives both to the usual way of doing business and/or as a different way of providing public services? There was by no means agreement between all of our interviewees on whether or when these alternatives would actually materialise, or how they would do so. It was, however, interesting to note that many of our interviewees were suggesting social enterprises could *replace, supplement* or *influence* mainstream businesses to provide a more human, more accountable and more equitable way of providing goods and services. Other benefits were described as providing more meaning or dignity for people in their work, or in the support they receive, than in the current system that focuses on profit-maximisation or financially-measured judgements about utility.

Each interview piece in the Voices section was necessarily selective. The authors and interviewees discussed and revised each piece so that it centred around an issue of concern that we both agreed had emerged from the hour-long interview. This left some interesting common concerns and turns of phrase out of the Voices section, that were nevertheless apparent to the authors. One of these surprising connections was just how many of our interviewees referred to Wilkinson and Pickett's *The spirit level:Why equality is better for everyone* and Stiglitz's *The price of inequality* as touchstones for the impact social enterprise approaches could have on society. These recent bestselling books describe how the vast inequality of both wealth and opportunity possible under the current capitalist system undermines democracy, justice and well-being and damages society for all – rich and poor. In referencing these books a number of our interviewees were acknowledging their aims for social enterprises as far broader than their specific type of business or current social purpose.

In their individual visions for the future it can be seen that social enterprise practitioners are aiming to improve upon existing service provision, enter new markets with more relevant products for disadvantaged groups or to redistribute wealth within specific geographic areas. Yet it is interesting to note that all of these goals seem to be compatible with the broader movement towards what has been called 'new' or 'human' economics (see for instance Boyle and Simms, 2009 and Hart et al, 2010 for excellent overviews of these fields) where proponents urge us to remember that money is a tool for exchange, for storing value, and for creating new objects or experiences of worth, not an end in itself.

Reformists and radicals

John Pearce's *Social enterprise in Anytown* described at least nine important ways in which social enterprises differ, including many of the points of difference already discussed above such as size, proportion of trading income, individual or collective orientation, voluntary or paid staff, focused or varied business activities, and also whether their social intent was what he called 'radical' or 'reformist' (2003, p44). This last spectrum referred to the extent to which social enterprises wanted to offer ways of changing the fabric of the current economic, political or cultural environment (radical) or alternatively focused on improving people's lot and solving problems within the current climate (reformist) as the route to change.

In the face of these multiple points of difference it is therefore important to make sure that discussions of social enterprise – whether in practice, policy or academia – are not reduced simply to debating how much trading income an organisation could or should earn in order to be thought of as a social enterprise and remain sustainable, or whether or not it is a good idea for voluntary and community organisations to think in a more 'business-like' way. It should be of concern to the sector that the UK political debate around social enterprises has often only been in reference to the role they can play in delivering public services, rather than being joined up to discussions in the wake of the financial crisis on the nature and purpose of business itself or even in relation to more meaningful citizen engagement, democracy and participation.

Campaigners for co-operation and **community development** and critical thinkers about the social economy undoubtedly remained aware of and debated wider political and philosophical issues – with European thinkers seemingly touching more often on these issues than those in the US. The EMES approach to understanding social enterprises, which encompasses the role of participatory governance *as well as* economic and social change dimensions (Defourney and Nyssens, 2010) is an illustration of this difference. Yet, ideas relating to power, social context, radicalism and authentic grassroots engagement have remained the focus of the few rather than the many in the broader social enterprise debate.

This has recently led some commentators (for example Dey and Steyaert, 2012) to highlight the extent to which these debates have been side-lined in favour of examining a supposedly apolitical vision of the *usefulness* of social enterprises within the systems and structures of society in which we currently find ourselves. In this book we are offering a different narrative, inquiring beyond a bland idea of *usefulness,* into the ideas on which social enterprise action is based, accepting that this must sit within a political context.

Despite the trend towards an apolitical debate, we have seen in the Voices section that many of those operating within the social enterprise sector in the UK are, to a greater or lesser extent, pursuing goals which have political implications.

We learnt of their specific goals, in arenas as different as revolutionising social care, financial services, leisure services, telecommunications and many others. However, when asked to look to the future, many of our Voices focused on broader goals: the role social enterprises could play in tackling inequality and on humanising the economy.

Altering from within or providing alternatives

While most of the interviewees in this book would argue that they are both pro-enterprise and socially minded at once, if we return to Pearce's ideas of reform and radicalism, we can see how the broader causes mentioned earlier can be pursued differently in practice. We want to highlight this difference because it provides a strong story of the different ways the social enterprise movement could influence the lives of people in the UK in the future. Our interviews suggested that some practitioners and thinkers hold aspirations both at the extremes of the spectrum of radical and reformist goals and, more often, in combinations of both. As clarity of purpose is often helpful when attempting to achieve change, the following discussion is intended to help readers to clarify their own positions on how and why they could or should be involved with the sector. The model below takes these ideas to extremes, in the hope that it will illuminate all the real life examples that of course fall somewhere in between.

Altering from within

In the future, social enterprises attempting to alter business and public services from within – Pearce's 'reformists' – will be those that focus on innovation, on productive partnerships and on gaining respect for the introduction of key ideas into the business mainstream. These involve introducing social value and social accountability to business practice and innovation and entrepreneurialism into the public and charitable sectors. Due to their focus on innovation and flexible responses to particular situations, reformists are more likely to resist definition and talk instead of breaking down boundaries between sectors so that definitions matter less. They will describe what they do as social entrepreneurship, social business, social innovation and just a new type of good business practice. They will be focused on the outcomes and impact of the business activities they undertake and in the functionality of any particular approach to governance, accountability or user involvement that they adopt. A focus on impact means that they will be more oriented towards the type of scale and awareness of social enterprises that comes with individual businesses expanding their operations into new geographic areas and greater use of contractual relationships between local government and social enterprises to make a difference in public services.

The great possibility that reformists offer in the future is of change in the wider economy by a broad and slow infiltration of ideas. By raising consumer awareness into thinking about social value, they make businesses more customer responsive and ethical, which then raises the bar for more mainstream businesses. In ideal circumstances, the focus they place on assessing the real outcomes of their work and transparently reporting on them, demonstrates ways to do this assessment accurately, so that more mainstream organisations can use these approaches. By working from within, they are stealthy and less threatening to the established order than vocal opponents – what Pearce calls the 'radicals' – who may cause defenders of traditional economic approaches to recoil and entrench.

Some of the activities that could be suggested to fit within this reformist agenda can be found in ideas covered by Shaun Doran, Matt Stevenson-Dodd and Jean Jarvis. All three are involved in delivering goods and services that transform people's lives and are providing exemplars of how to deliver public service contracts in a more holistic way to provide long-term solutions to society's problems. They provide illustrations of how, by responding with awareness to pressing current needs and by drawing innovative combinations of currently available resources together, services can be improved, jobs can be created for disadvantaged people and better living environments can be created.

Barriers to the future of reformist approaches include the widespread cynicism, expressed by many of the Voices, over organisations attempting to, in the words of one of our interviewees 'wear the clothes' of social and environmentally active organisations, without following through with genuinely transformative actions. While our contributors are clearly working within the bounds of genuine social enterprise, some people worry that in a sector without clear definitions and required value statements, other businesses could easily adopt the language of social innovation without facing the reporting, governance or legal conventions that would reveal the real nature and impact of the businesses. At worst, reformist organisations could end up as a legitimising face and provide window dressing for continuing the excesses of free market capitalism. By cherry-picking only the features of more radical models that are palatable to current norms of business and capitalism they could miss the point of using business as a tool for greater empowerment, democratic involvement and redistribution of power and wealth within society (Mayo, 2011).

Of course, this worst case scenario need not become reality. We draw on the knowledge of the Voices to assert that avoiding it will require strong individual *and* collective leadership, great use of communications technology to spread the message, a clear vision of the extent to which the economy might be required to change to support further reforms, long-term commitment, clarity on where lines of principle should be drawn, and where accountability and transparency should be genuinely embedded in all areas of the businesses' activities.

Providing alternatives

In the future, radical social enterprises attempting to provide an alternative to mainstream businesses and the current arrangements for public services will be those which support distinctions that embed collective or more accountable ways of managing into their governing documents. They will focus on challenging preconceptions about the purpose of business and the 'naturalness' of doing business in particular ways. They will seek to gain respect for ideas of working collectively and in communities, through self-help and mutuality, for the value of networks of people and on the quality and relevance of the goods or services they provide. They are radical because they are not claiming to be 'business as usual' with a social twist, but instead they try to convey how the production of quality outcomes is tied up in power, alternative governance and management processes and the genuine transformation of micro and macro economies.

As they are part of broader movements for environmental change, democratic processes and human scale activity, they are more likely to welcome definitions that provide clarity over the values and philosophy underpinning their approaches. They will describe what they do as social enterprise, co-operation, community development and solidarity economics. They will draw on a rich history of explorations into employee ownership, collective governance and participative democracy. They will draw on and develop existing templates for how to bring people together and help them to help themselves, through taking a vote or a stake in the business that will change things for themselves and their communities. Because they see process as part and parcel of providing change they are oriented towards the type of scale and awareness of social enterprises that comes with individual businesses either creating franchises in new geographic areas with the involvement of local people, or the proliferation of business activities within one geographic area interlinked for greater effectiveness. They are wary of attempts to change the means of delivering public services unless decent safeguards for participative governance and accountability are in place although they see great potential for a more direct kind of democratic involvement in services if these safeguards could be provided.

The great possibility that radical social enterprises offer in the future is in providing robust challenges to the existing hegemony of profit-driven, shareholder capitalism and offering good examples that demonstrate how things can be done differently. They will seek to lead consumer awareness of the variety of ways in which organising and working together can lead to better outcomes for all, particularly through providing bespoke, people-centred goods and services. Reversing the current distinction between owners of organisations and customers, they can create ways to make all organisations more accountable and society more equal. By challenging the system, they are visible, provocative and therefore sometimes are found operating outside (intentionally or because they are kept out) more influential and powerful circles that reformists might be able to inhabit.

Examples of elements of radicalism include when Malcolm Hayday talks about the way financial institutions could be transformed to provide genuine alternatives to the mainstream. Graham Wiles describes a 'circular economy' that integrates and caters to the needs of people and the environment together in a way that current supply and demand thinking simply cannot. Iain Tuckett describes how an inner city area was transformed by local residents taking on ownership of their community, rather than allowing remote developers the power over their locality.

Barriers to the future of radical organisations include practical concerns over how effective collective leadership and involvement can be. At worst, groups of people start these types of organisation with the good intentions but can find it difficult to work together in a society that has grown increasingly oriented towards individualism. Without easily available current examples of where and how co-operation has flourished before, for example, through membership of mutual building societies, friendly societies and trade unions, it is not always possible for people to learn about the value of sticking with some of the challenges of co-operation, collaboration and genuine involvement. Some established techniques for joint decision making, consultation and equitable sharing of rewards are unknown in some newer social enterprises, where people then struggle to reinvent them. Radical social enterprises can also suffer from idealism getting in the way of making enough money to be sustainable and therefore to contribute anything at all – what Tim Smit succinctly calls being made "un-robust by hippyness".

Although this characterisation of radical social enterprise may seem very different to the reformist one above, we discern from the Voices that avoiding these pitfalls will largely require the same safeguards as described above. There is no reason why attempts that involve elements of radicalism should not be taken seriously, just as reformist approaches need not necessarily be subverted. It will take strong individual *and* collective leadership, great use of communications technology to spread the message, a clear vision of the extent to which the economy might be required to change to promote these radical aims, long-term commitment, clarity on where lines of principle should be drawn and where it is possible to be flexible, and genuinely embed accountability, transparency and mutuality. Those making the case for promoting, supporting and developing social enterprises will need to focus on these similarities if they are to conceive the variety of models as a strength rather than a weakness.

The pictures of reformist and radical approaches given here have admittedly been exaggerated, if only to highlight the range of possibilities open to the social enterprise movement. Yet even then, our interpretation of what is required by the movement that encompasses these approaches is virtually the same – if it can be recognised that it is a movement towards reducing inequality and humanising the economy. However, there is one key difference in the future prospects of these approaches that must be highlighted here. While the current economic and cultural order encourages entrepreneurialism and individual endeavour (compatible with the reformist model of social enterprise where ideas slowly filter into the mainstream), there is a danger that in a culture geared largely towards individualised ideas of self, success, self-fulfilment or personal failure, working in groups is becoming harder and harder. This could make the future more challenging for the part of the radical model of social enterprise that is grounded in collective action. Raising awareness of this issue is part of the solution to combatting it.

The specifics of improving the quality of life for people in the UK

The two futures described above are extreme examples, rather than real predictions of how things could turn out. In reality, it is likely that a mix of radical provocation and change from within (even operating within the same organisations) will work together to alter the economy in ways we can't yet see. Of course, other forces such as environmental and technological change, global politics and international agreements will all also contribute to making current predictions inaccurate. Yet the act of predicting has value for our own time. Just as science fiction visions of the future from films and television inevitably tell us more about the mores and hopes of the times in which they were made than providing realistic predictions, these interviews looking to the future have given us the means of exploring a wide range of current ideas and values.

Many of our Voices have valuable things to say about key issues that will concern us in the coming years: Margaret Elliot talks about transforming the quality of care services, Tim Smit discusses environmental sustainability and Jenny Sims describes creating jobs for those who have been excluded from the labour market. When reading each of the interviews we are reminded of the individual passions and social preoccupations that populate the social enterprise sector.

While the discussion above has focused on the larger jigsaw – the movement towards humanising the economy – in which the social enterprise piece could comprise a major or central part, we must not lose sight of the fact that individual social enterprises are often not set up with this goal explicitly in mind. They respond to particular needs, to social issues, to defined problems and to unfulfilled aspirations within communities and localities. This section has not been an attempt to argue that these preoccupations are unimportant – far from it. The everyday, practical improvements that these organisations provide to individuals and groups are their lifeblood. Without specific divergent preoccupations and goals, the general movement would undoubtedly not exist. Instead, by interpreting the social enterprise movement in this way we hope to highlight how seemingly disparate specific activities like creating a fish farm on a bus and operating

215

Olympic legacy sports venues can co-exist, support and learn from each other within a movement for change.

Towards clarity

In the introduction it was suggested that the most basic level, social enterprises are organisations which:

- sell goods or services to obtain at least some of their income;
- carry out activities that are socially or environmentally beneficial;
- write their governing documents in a way that makes clear the social intent behind the business (to benefit people and/or the environment).

Additionally, some social enterprises emphasise that they:

- do not distribute their profits for private benefit;
- are owned by people who have a stake in the business, such as working in it, buying from it or living in the local community.

In this overview we have gone further than this fairly cool and clinical description to suggest that there is a more insightful way of looking at social enterprises. They can be seen as organisations that involve strongly held (explicit or implicit) political and social beliefs and priorities and therefore debate and critical engagement are not only likely but absolutely vital. From this point of view the common complaint that the sector is always disagreeing with itself is actually a source of richness and potential. By disagreeing, people are looking beyond a standardised view of what is *useful* and making sure to ask the key ethical questions required by any human action: *in what context are they or could they be useful, what does useful mean, to whom* and *by what means?*

It is therefore important to this richer view of social enterprise to recognise that social enterprises are guided by specific aims to help people, the environment and communities and that these aims can be varied and diverse. They are guided by commitments to particular methods, processes or ways of interacting and these can also be quite different from one another. They can be pieced into different political agendas and wider movements for social change. Yet we should remember these uses and impressions of social enterprise are not 'natural', 'inevitable' or outside of the control of the sector or those who might enter it in the future. By achieving greater clarity on specific and general goals and value commitments, we argue, the sector will be better able to shape its own future rather than become dependent on short-term political objectives in an ever-changing policy environment. We have learned from our Voices that, however different individual approaches may be, many people and organisations do share the goal of trying to make their world a better place by doing better business – creating a social enterprise movement for the future.

Appendix One

The future of social enterprise: a contradictory agenda for change

The following is an agenda for change – drawing on the ideas of our interviewees and offering thoughts on what could help or hinder social enterprise development. Many of the suggestions are contradictory. Yet, as we have established, these contradictions could be key in debates on the future of social enterprise. We suggest that clarity over where there is potential for disagreement can only help start and inform those debates. For this reason, a wide range of potential actions have been presented below.

Actions for NATIONAL GOVERNMENT

- define social enterprises (or particular sub-types of social enterprises like employee-owned businesses or **social firms**) in order to provide tax breaks or other incentives to their formation and growth;
- withdraw from influencing the social enterprise definition debate and allow the sector itself to define or not define itself as it wishes;
- change the laws around financial institutions to allow the credit union movement to expand;
- make it easier to set up businesses using community shares, or a combination of community shares and private investment;
- go further than the current **Social Value Act** in requiring local government to contract on the basis of broader concepts of value than lowest cost or financial measures of best value;
- provide funding for business support that helps start-ups and developing organisations in a way that takes into consideration that some businesses might trade for a social purpose;

- take a more active stance in ensuring the beneficial impact on society and environment of all businesses – whether social enterprises or not.

Actions for LOCAL GOVERNMENT

- involve social enterprises in the commissioning of public services to make sure good ideas in the **third sector** are acknowledged and promoted through public sector choices;
- learn from the development processes of existing successful social enterprises, rather than re-inventing the wheel, spinning out their own versions;
- promote the assessment of broader concepts of value in all of their contractors, particularly learning from the example of social enterprises.

Actions for INFRASTRUCTURE ORGANISATIONS (networks, membership and lobbying groups)

- lobby for opportunities to contract for public services;
- get closer to existing mainstream businesses and promote partnerships and exchanges of talent and ideas;
- lobby for better social enterprise education in schools and higher education;
- lobby for more appropriate 'patient' finance opportunities;
- provide certification for 'real' social enterprises;
- sell the idea of social enterprise on quality;
- sell the idea of social enterprise on ethics.

Actions for SCHOOLS AND THE HIGHER EDUCATION SYSTEM

- provide more than just a single mention of trading for purposes other than private profit-maximisation in the GCSE and A-level curriculums;
- better explain how politics and values influence the economic system we currently have so that students can understand how they could differ;
- offer opportunities for genuinely collective decision-making and action.

Actions for CONSUMERS

- accept that each of their purchasing decisions holds the power to change how business is carried out;
- consider the priorities they give to making purchasing decisions on the basis of ethics, quality and cost;
- spread awareness of the potential of social enterprises.

Actions for SOCIAL ENTERPRISES: clarify which of the following best reflect the values and aims of their organisation

- work to provide the best quality products and services in their business sector;
- work to reduce their costs and make their products accessible to more people;
- publicise their ethics and their alternative way of doing business;
- let the quality of their services speak for itself;
- grow by expanding existing operations into new geographical areas;
- grow by expanding into different business activities in the same geographic area;
- grow by franchising their model and helping others to follow their lead;
- grow slowly with a focus on retaining quality of governance and involvement;
- grow fast by designing the business by adapting ideas from the business mainstream;
- train people from the community to fill their job positions;
- attract high-flyers who would otherwise have gone into mainstream business or the civil service;
- seek large contributions of outside investment that expect a return with interest;
- seek smaller and more collective ways of gaining investment;
- consider how they affect only the disadvantaged people whom they are designed to help;
- consider how they affect the full range of **stakeholders** with whom they engage.

Appendix Two

Interview schedule and questions used for this research

Thank you for agreeing to be interviewed. This is going to be an unusual interview in that what we are trying to do is draw out your idea of what social enterprises – either your own or the sector in general – could be doing 20 years into the future. We're not just asking for a reasoned and realistic forecast – although you can give us that if you'd like. We're looking for what you think social enterprise could or should be 20 years down the line. We're looking for what we call: Future Visions.

Once we've interviewed you, we'll take away your answers and try to write up a small story on your future vision. We'll send it back to you to check that it represents what you want it to, making any changes necessary until it's right.

First of all – we'd like to ask two introductory questions, so that we are familiar with your current work and stance. These are different if you a run a social enterprise yourself to if you support a social enterprise, research them or advise them.

Do-ers

- What is your social enterprise's mission and how are you delivering on that mission?
- What support or information have you received to help you specifically with social enterprise start-up or development?

Thinkers/supporters

- What is your personal working definition of 'social enterprise' (Note: we are not looking for a long definitional debate here, just a sentence or two on your everyday understanding of social enterprise)?

- What support or information do you think is necessary for social enterprise start-up or development? Have you been involved in providing any of this?

Now we're going to ask you questions to help you think about your vision:

- What do you want your social enterprise/the social enterprise sector to do in the future?
- Who do you want to own social enterprises, run them and work for them? That is, who should have involvement with social enterprises?
- Where will the boundaries of the public and private sectors be – or will there be no boundaries?
- Will social enterprise become a mainstream way of doing business, understood by the general public?
- Can you foresee any issues or dangers that might subvert people's understanding of social enterprise?
- Is any kind of support/information/policy necessary to overcome these dangers?
- Crucially, what difference could all this make to the quality and experience of people's lives in the UK?

Then, building on your answers to the previous question, we're going to talk through your vision in concrete terms – who, how, when, where, why. This will help us build the story, and the process will be individual to each Future Vision.

References

Boyle, D, Simms, A, 2009, *The new economics: A bigger picture,* London and New York: Earthscan

Chew, C, Lyon, F, 2012, Innovation and social enterprise activity in third sector organisations, *Third Sector Research Centre Working Paper Series* 83, Birmingham: TSRC

Co-operative Commission, 2001, *The co-operative advantage: Creating a successful family of co-operative businesses*, www.co-opcommission.org.uk

Defourney, J, 2009, Foreword, in J Kerlin (ed) *Social enterprise: A global comparison*, Medford, MA: Tufts University Press, pxi–pxvi

Defourney, J, Nyssens, M, 2010, Social enterprise, in K Hart, JL Laville, AD Cattani (eds) *The human economy: A citizen's guide,* Cambridge: Polity Press, 284–92

Dey, P, Steyaert, C, 2012, Social entrepreneurship: Critique and the radical enactment of the social, *Social Enterprise Journal* 8, 2, 90–107

Dey, P, Teasdale, S, 2013, Social enterprise and dis/identification: The politics of identity work in the English third sector, *Administrative theory and praxis* 35, 2, 248–70

DTI (Department for Trade and Industry), 2002, *Social enterprise: A strategy for success,* London: HMSO

Foote, N, Eisenstat, R, Fredberg, T, 2011, The higher ambition leader, *Harvard Business Review* September, 94–101

Friedman, M, 1970. The social responsibility of business is to increase its profits, *The New York Times Magazine* 13 September

Hart, K, Laville, JL, Cattani, AD (eds) 2010, *The human economy: A citizen's guide*, Cambridge: Polity Press

International Co-operative Alliance, 2013, *Blueprint for a co-operative decade*, www.ica.coop

Lettice, F, Parekh, M, 2010, The social innovation process: Themes, challenges and implications for practice, *International Journal of Technology Management* 51, 1, 139–58

McKay, S, Moro, D, Teasdale, S, Clifford, D, 2011, The marketisation of charities in England and Wales, *Third Sector Research Centre Working Paper Series* 69, Birmingham: TSRC

Mayo, E, 2011, The hidden alternative: Conclusion, in A Webster, L Shaw, JK Walton, A Brown, D Stewart (eds) *The hidden alternative: Co-operative values past, present and future*, Manchester: Manchester University Press

Nicholls, 2008, *Social enterpreneurship: New models of sustainable social change*, Oxford: Oxford University Press

Palmer, H., Mornement, A, 2005, *From asking to earning: Experiences of trading* [Report], Exeter: RISE

Pearce, J, 2003, *Social enterprise in Anytown*, London: Calouste Gulbenkian Foundation

Porter, ME, Kramer, MR, 2011, Creating shared value, *Harvard Business Review* January–February, 62–77

SEUK (Social Enterprise UK), 2013, *The people's business: State of social enterprise survey 2013*, www.socialenterprise.org.uk

Stiglitz, JE, 2012, *The price of inequality: How today's divided society endangers our future*, New York: W.W. Norton

Teasdale, S, Kerlin, J, Young, D, In Soh, J, 2013a, Oil and water rarely mix: Exploring the relative stability of non-profit revenue mixes over time, *Journal of Social Entrepreneurship* 4, 1, 69–87

Teasdale, S, Lyon, F, Baldock, R, 2013b, Playing with numbers: A methodological critique of the social enterprise growth myth, *Journal of Social Entrepreneurship* 4, 2, 113–31

Wilkinson, R, Pickett, K, 2010, *The spirit level: Why equality is better for everyone*, London: Penguin Books

Yunus, M, Weber, K, 2010, *Building social business: A new kind of capitalism that serves humanity's most pressing needs*, New York: Public Affairs

Index

Note: names in bold type refer to 'Voices'.